Hearing-impaired children under five

a guide for parents and teachers

*dedicated to
the memory of
Irene R Ewing*

Sir Alexander Ewing
&
Lady Ethel C Ewing

Hearing-impaired children under five

a guide for parents and teachers

Manchester University Press

USA:
The Volta Bureau, Washington

© 1971 Sir Alexander Ewing & Lady Ethel C. Ewing

All rights reserved

Published by Manchester University Press
316-324 Oxford Road, Manchester M13 9NR

ISBN 0 7190 0466 7

U.S.A.
The Volta Bureau
1537 35th Street, N.W. Washington, D.C. 20007

Printed in Great Britain by
William Clowes & Sons, Limited
London, Beccles and Colchester

Contents

List of figures

Preface

Our chief aim in writing this book has been to make available, in detail and in their most up-to-date form, our methods for helping infants and very young children with impaired hearing to understand speech and to talk, beginning at the earliest possible age. We have in mind all those in different countries who share, in some way, responsibility for these children. Our two life-times of thought and actual practice have left us completely convinced that for a majority of deaf and hard-of-hearing children under five their parents are the key figures. Our deepest sympathy goes out to the parents and the children themselves in the tasks that lie ahead. For the sake of parents we have done our best to present all our information in non-technical language. But also we hope that it can be of assistance to professional workers, teachers of the deaf and audiologists, especially those who undertake parent guidance. The chapter that gives a fully detailed description of our procedures for making screening tests of children aged seven months to five years will be useful, we hope, to medical officers, health visitors and public health nurses.

Developments in scientific thinking in recent years, for instance in linguistics and communication theory as well as in acoustics and technology, continue to offer better understanding of the children's needs and greater facilities for meeting them. By reporting what particular parents and their children, in all their different conditions, said and did we have tried to present the application of present-day knowledge in real life situations.

Our most grateful thanks go to Professor I. G. Taylor of the Department of Audiology and Education of the Deaf, University of Manchester, for access to the resources of his Department. We wish to thank Mr. J. E. J. John, Lecturer in Audiology, for reviewing with us the diagrams included in Chapter Six, also Mr. A. Kettlety, Senior Experimental Officer, for laboratory tests of apparatus. The manuscript was typed by Mrs. B. M. J. Whittaker.

A.W.G.E.
E.C.E.

    Horseshoe Cottage
    Alderley Edge
    Cheshire

1
Recognising problems and needs

We begin this book of methods by offering reports on nine hearing-impaired children, how they were found, diagnosed and assessed and how their parents were guided to help them. There were considerable variations, of course, in their handicaps, among their parents and in their home conditions. One common factor was the co-operative effort by parents, audiologists and teachers to enable them to learn to talk during the first five years of life, no matter how profoundly deaf reliable modern testing showed them to be. An essential factor was the early medical diagnosis of their handicap.

We hope that, by quoting some of the details of what happened, step by step, in individual cases, we are providing a realistic approach to our whole system of parent guidance. Most of our evidence comes from reports, written after individual guidance sessions—usually fortnightly—in the University of Manchester Clinic—and from intensive study of tape recordings. To play and replay these recordings of mothers training their children is a fascinating way of re-creating real-life situations, often at different stages in the progress of both children and parents. All of them were known to one or both of us.

Jane
Jane was one of those children who are, unfortunately, profoundly deaf, with that great handicap coming as a bolt out of the blue. The consultant otologist diagnosed it as due to an unknown cause. She had been born in hospital. There was no report of any ante-natal or peri-natal abnormality. Fortunately for her she was referred to Manchester University Audiology Clinic at the age of

1 year 6 months. It had been noted previously that she was making no response to sound and that when she wanted things her almost sole means of communication was to point to them. She vocalised very little and had no understanding of speech. Later, pure-tone audiometry confirmed a hearing loss averaging 93 decibels in the better ear.

Jane's parents showed wisdom and courage in accepting the medical diagnosis of her deafness and its extent, when demonstrated to them. They accepted her need of daily home training and hearing-aid amplification under regular individual guidance from the University clinic, with the extra time and effort that that would involve. The home could be described as "stable middle-class". Jane had a brother (not deaf) a few years older than herself.

Age 1 year 8 months. After one month of home training, Jane was watching faces very well and vocalising very freely with varied intonation.

Both parents became very active in home training and gave it a high priority. They learnt quickly what was wanted for their child and set out to achieve it. A speech training hearing aid was used, in the clinic at first, and the very marked increase in the quantity and quality of Jane's vocalisations seemed to follow soon after the initiation of this. Within two months Jane fully accepted use of an individual hearing aid and by 2 years 9 months would not be parted from it. She reacted sharply to voice heard through it at four to five feet.

Jane began to try to talk after four months of home training, just before she was two years old. She was attempting to say a few words, e.g. "ee" (teeth). In her attempts to imitate speech Jane used other appropriate vowels and consonants.

Age 2 years 8 months. After twelve months of home training, Jane was saying imperfectly but recognisably "thank you, hello, mumma, babba, out, hot, bye-bye, ah". Seven months later still Jane was observed to be talking to herself in solitary play. This would seem to be clear evidence that a voice to ear link, of which there was none before home training, had been established and that, by now, Jane had come to hear her own voice without thinking about it. In both communicative situations and solitary play words were interspersed with jargon. She was beginning to use sounds gained at least partly by hearing, e.g. /k/ in "Keith" and

/d/ in familiar words. After a further two months of home training she was using "motor" and "pussy" among her new words.

Jane was admitted to the Nursery-Infant School for the Deaf,
of which I (E.C.E.) had charge, at the age of 3 years 7 months.
Her speech was easily intelligible to the teachers, as well as to her
parents, but not easily understood by strangers. Like most normally hearing children, at this stage, she understood much more
than she could say.

At the age of seven years, when tested in vocabulary and spoken
language, she was ahead of deaf children of similar age and intelligence who had had no home training. Her intelligence was
tested with the Raven Coloured Matrices and found to be
Grade II, average.

Sally

It was at her parents' request that Sally was referred to the
University Clinic. When, at the age of 1 year 2 months, she was
neither vocalising nor understanding any speech, they were concerned about her hearing. Of their other four children one was
deaf and attending a school for the deaf. There had been a
difficult birth in both cases of deafness.

Free-field diagnostic testing showed that Sally could just hear a
male voice at a sound level of 65 decibels, i.e. the maximum level
reached in moderately loud conversation at three feet. For some
of the higher pitched sound essential to the hearing of many
consonants, e.g. /s/, she was profoundly deaf. Subsequent pure-
tone audiograms at 3 years 3 months and later confirmed this
patterning of high-tone deafness. These audiograms have shown
no air-bone gap, which would account for the absence of spontaneous vocalisation before home training with amplification was
begun.[1]

Sally's mother was a busy farmer's wife but she contrived to
make time to give her a good deal of home training every day.
Under guidance she became outstandingly skilful and successful
in so doing.

Age 1 year 11 months. Sally understood about forty words and
used about twenty. She also spoke a lot of jargon with good voice
quality. By that time her parents had become skilled in speaking
at a voice level suitable for reception by a hearing aid user—with

[1] An audiogram of Sally is illustrated and discussed in Chapter Six.

clear articulation and the speed, rhythm and phrasing suitable for a small deaf child. Besides a wearable hearing aid a speech training aid—i.e. auditory training unit—was in regular daily use. The parents had gathered quite good toy material for use in training periods, suitable for gaining interest and evoking speech but needed help in learning how to use it. Sally's tiny but growing expressive vocabulary, at this stage, included such words as "man, tractor, train", learnt in the contrived play situations. Normally, for speech reception, she relied on combining lipreading with what she could hear of amplified sound.

Age 2 years 7 months. By this time Sally had begun to put words together, for instance "daddy's tractor", "baby calf", "that's daddy's pig", "I don't know". Her articulation varied with different words, e.g. for "wheel" she said /ee/ but the phrases quoted above were said very clearly. A key point of the guidance given to all parents at our clinic was that from the very beginning of home training they should speak to their hearing-impaired children in phrases and short sentences. As Sally's own utterances increasingly illustrated, colloquialisms were encouraged.

Age 3 years 6 months. Now, after rather more than two years' home training and, no doubt, with increasing maturation, Sally's vocabulary was growing very quickly. At this period, in play with small toys, a tape recording shows her to have said spontaneously "that's for that one", "there another white chair", "ladying feeding the hens", "bird going to sit on tree", "put tree in road", "sit in the wheelbarrow", "another hou(s)e in garden", "no horn and baby calf lying down", "wash hair in the ba(th)", "(t)raffi(c) light—red", "daddy pig ugh ugh". By the time that Sally had reached this stage in learning to talk it had become clear that the severity of her deafness to high tones was interfering with her acquisition of such consonants as /s/ and /th/. There were a good many examples in addition to those quoted above. For "spade" Sally said "'pade", for "bus" "bu'", for "nice", "ni'", etc.

Transcriptions and tape recordings of Sally's spontaneous utterances were made at this stage. In one session, for instance, she spoke a total number of 387 words. Of these 100 were different words, many of which she had used several times. A grammatical analysis of the different words gave 53 nouns, 10 verbs, 16 adjectives, 3 prepositions, 1 conjunction, 2 articles, 3 particles, 6 pronouns and 6 adverbs. Just over half of her utterances consisted of two or three words, 35 per cent of single words and 14 per cent of four or five words. After careful consideration it was felt that Sally's mother should be advised to use more verbs and a greater variety of them. Transcriptions made fourteen and seventeen months later showed that this was effective—e.g. "they can't drink the brook, she's sitting on the stool, you don't need a fence, laughing at the cow, he jumped and the cat jumped, I don't want that, can you find the shippon? I think he's got to stop in the fields." At 4 years 11 months, out of a series of 31 utterances 30 included a verb.

Tom

When Tom, an only child, was eighteen months old he was referred to the out-patient clinic in the Ear, Nose and Throat Department of a teaching hospital. His parents had asked for this. Tom was not talking and they "thought he might be slightly deaf". The consultant otologist who examined him found nothing that would indicate a cause of deafness. The baby responded to loud noises near his ears. Tom was referred from the hospital to the Manchester University Audiology Clinic. Tests confirmed a considerable degree of deafness in both ears. There was auditory acuity throughout the range of pitch needed to hear speech well, but voice and other sound evoked no response unless their loudness level was above 70 decibels, i.e. appreciably louder than ordinary conversation or than teachers generally talk in school. The deafness on the left side was greater than this, with the effect that when Tom did hear sound he did not localise its direction. An audiogram, made at the age of 3 years 10 months, confirmed this.

Tom had a very modest home background. His father was troubled by a stammer. The mother took the initiative. An essential need for successful home training—establishment of a good and happy mother–child relationship—took a long time to develop. This was a case in which eventually good results were achieved through training in the home in spite of difficulties. At the outset Tom's mother thought he was slow in every way. His general development was somewhat delayed, sitting at nine months, not walking without support until eighteen months. When he was only fourteen months old, Tom's mother would have liked to put him into a nursery.

5

Tom had a hearing aid from the age of 1 year 8 months. There were initial difficulties about supplying him with accurately fitting ear-moulds and in interesting him sufficiently in sound to gain his acceptance of wearing an aid. After five months of home training, however, Tom was seen to enjoy listening to sound. Indeed, he would put many things up to his ears, apparently expecting to hear sound coming from them.

Progress at first was slow. The mother needed much encouragement and support. In the earlier months she had to be asked to speak to Tom more slowly and distinctly. Brief demonstrations of use of toys in such a way as to win his co-operation were frequently necessary. It was when Tom's mother learnt to be skilful in attracting his attention to her face, so that he could combine lipreading with use of a hearing aid, that his understanding of what she said to him began to grow.

Age 2 years 4 months. Tom was understanding up to twenty words and phrases such as "bye-bye, doggy, aeroplane, pussy cat, biscuit, bubbles, bird, ball, good boy". Some words like these he was attempting to say, although as yet most of his spontaneous efforts at communication took the form of jargon. Much greater variety in the tones of his voice was now noted.

Age 3 years. By this time Tom was attempting to use a wider vocabulary. In a tape recording he is heard to try to say "(h)ere(s) a ba(ll), i(ce) (c)ream(m), u(m)brella, towe(l), mifo (microphone)". At this age he tried to say "knife, fork, spoon, pan".

The increasing extent to which Tom's articulation of consonants was developing while his mother was using a speech training hearing aid with him, at home, was carefully analysed. The method used was to make tape recordings of consecutive utterances by him which the guider judged to be meaningful. In the six months after Tom reached the age of three years he had acquired fifteen consonants. Whereas at the beginning of the period he used chiefly /b/, /w/, /l/ by the end of that time his utterances included /p/, /m/, /d/, /n/, /k/, /g/, /r/, /h/, as well as approximations to some other consonants. Whereas the recording at the beginning of the period showed Tom to be saying only single words, the one six months later included twelve phrases and sentences which were intelligible to the parent or worker. Perhaps it should be made clear that no formal articulation teaching of any kind was being included in Tom's home

6

training. His use of an increased variety of consonants (also of vowels and diphthongs) seems to have been the product, despite his very severe deafness, of his home training with the speech trainer in combination with lipreading. Development of a useful degree of auditory discrimination seems to be indicated. Later when almost five years old, Tom could put in almost all consonants, including /s/, when he listened carefully through the speech trainer. A psychological report stated that by that time he could discriminate words and phrases, well known to him, by listening alone.

Transcription of a recording of Tom with his mother when he was 4 years 10 months old illustrates both how far he had got in learning to talk and also his great need of further expert education. Spontaneously he said "umbrella kree (green), drivin' a car, teddy bear in bed and go(ll)ywo(g) in bed, two pengui(ns), (g)iraffe, teddy bear in bed wi(th) gir(l), baby cow and mummy cow, one, two, tree, four, five (in answer to mummy's how many?), yellow butterfly".

At the age of five years Tom followed simple stories illustrated by pictures, asked questions, e.g. "what is it? can I have ... ?". He would relate past experiences and talk about future events.

Charlie

Charlie was only three months old when his deafness was first diagnosed by a hospital consultant. The reasons for so early a referral were, first, that he was known to belong to a "risk group" because his mother had caught rubella, german measles, from her other children ten weeks after Charlie was conceived. Then, no doubt because they knew that, as a result, the infant when born might be deaf, his parents observed that he did not respond to sound.

The otologist reported that, on examination, he found no abnormality of the ears. He obtained no response to very loud sounds. At a first visit to the Manchester University Clinic there was no definite indication that Charlie had any capacity to hear. It was through home training that he came to enjoy listening to amplified sound and benefited much from it when learning to talk, in spite of deafness that was shown to be profound on the right side and sub-total on the left.

Charlie's parents were not well-to-do but his mother stayed at home and was able to give him the kinds of home training that he needed. The home was in mid-Cheshire and after an initial period in the University Clinic, guidance to the parents was undertaken by members of the County's staff. At regular intervals we ourselves saw him in County Audiology Clinics.

Age 1 year 1 month. Already, at this early age, Charlie had become accustomed to periods of informal home training with the speech training hearing aid, lasting as long as twenty minutes. His mother was being guided to play a xylophone, ring little bells and beat a drum, with Charlie watching her and with a microphone of the speech trainer near the instrument that she was using. Charlie showed obvious enjoyment in this kind of play. His mother learnt to make the musical sounds rhythmical. It was through this approach that Charlie came to notice his mother's voice when amplified, first of all when she sang in time to the music. To do this she held a microphone near her mouth but not in such a way as at all to hide her face. Naturally, at this stage, his mother needed help in achieving good microphone techniques. One method was for her to wear the headset while the guider moved further and further away from the microphone and monitored her voice to maintain the same level of loudness. This was, of course, to demonstrate the need to speak close to the microphone. A second microphone was connected to the speech training aid and hung round Charlie's neck so that when, as a result of hearing his mother's voice and seeing her lips move, he began to use his own voice, he could hear that too amplified. Other noise-making toys were useful at this stage and, as young as he was, he began to imitate such ways of moving them as would enable him to make noises that he could hear through the speech trainer.

Age 1 year 2 months. Charlie had evidently begun to enjoy using his own voice, especially when imitating the way in which his mother zoomed as she pretended to fly a little aeroplane across the table towards him. In all these little games Charlie's mother became accustomed to say to him in sentences exactly what she was doing—e.g. "here's an aeroplane, I'll fly it to you".

Age 2 years. In the clinic, with little toys, Charlie responded correctly to simple requests such as "put the baby in the pram" and "put the dog on the chair". When doing this he was watching

8

the face of the speaker and using a super-power aid which he wore all day. His mother reported "He says quite a lot of words." Samples heard in the clinic were "cha(ir), pu(ff)-pu(ff), woo(f)-woo(f), miaow, ta (thank you)."

Age 2 years 10 months. Charlie was now making good attempts to talk in phrases and sentences with good rhythm but, not surprisingly, approximate articulation.

Charlie made such good progress in every way, socially as well as linguistically, that his parents desired to keep on with home training and not to send him to a nursery school for the deaf until he was nearly five years old. In a tape recording made at home his spontaneous utterances include short sentences and phrases such as "I got a wheel, big, big wheel, man tract (man on the tractor), that's the man car (that's the man in the cart), that got blue, that a culock (clock), open ee gor (open the door). I want feather (articulated very approximately), we(ll)ington(s)." When looking at a picture of chickens Charlie quite spontaneously vocalises "oo——pee" on a high-pitched, very pretty musical note. This appears to confirm that through constant use of amplification a very effective ear to voice link had been established.

Freda

When Freda was first referred to the University clinic she was 2 years 4 months old and not talking. Her mother had been diagnosed as having an attack of rubella—german measles—in the ninth week of the pregnancy. At the first test of Freda's hearing it was clear that on the one hand her deafness was very severe but that on the other hand she responded to loud sound over nearly the whole range of pitch involved in speech. At an early stage it became clear that to hear sound at all she was dependent on the right ear. When, much later, tests of hearing by bone conduction were made, responses could be obtained at what, for a clinical bone conduction receiver, is a high level of output—55–65 decibels.

The home was middle class—the father an engineer, the mother an ex-school-teacher of music. At the first guidance visit the mother reported that she had heard Freda use /b/, /m/, /n/, /d/ and /j/ when vocalising to herself. They had been taking and putting into practice the Tracy Clinic Correspondence Course and had also used the Ewings' book *New Opportunities for Deaf Children*.

Home visits by a member of the University staff just before regular guidance sessions in the clinic began revealed that Freda's mother was finding her very difficult indeed to handle. Establishment of mutual communication between mother and child was soon to reverse that situation. In spite of having a baby only a few months old Freda's mother made a rapid response to guidance and became outstandingly skilful and understanding of Freda's needs.

Age 2 years 11 months. Initial difficulties in persuading Freda to wear the headset of a speech training aid, for short periods, were being overcome. At a session in the University, while her mother was training her under guidance, she kept on the headset for thirty-five minutes. She vocalised freely into the microphone, beginning perhaps to imitate /ow/ when her mother said "cow". It was noteworthy that at this stage Freda always started to vocalise as soon as a hearing aid was put on. Her mother was already using a good clear voice to talk to her. She was advised always to put words into a sentence, however simple. She had gathered a good range of toys for her daily home sessions with the speech trainer. She reported that Freda had begun to say single words at home—"abble (apple), 'ain (rain), off".

Age 3 years 3 months. Freda's mother was becoming more skilful in planning and using play situations with the speech trainer. It was still not always easy to gain Freda's interest. The play had to be made "dramatic". The animals had to run into the stable. The cow had to jump. The lorry must be pushed along the road. Zoo animals were a great success. Not only was Freda's expressive vocabulary growing but she was now articulating a variety of consonants—"apple (now normally spoken), fwower (flower), tok (clock), bu-it (bucket), osh (horse), sun, tea, su-ar (sugar)". At this period Freda's mother wrote down the words that she heard her use and found that in seven weeks her vocabulary had grown from 78 to 221 words. Phrases were beginning to appear—"Himmy sheet (Timothy is asleep), slipper off, how ma(n)y, door shut, Mummy'(s) book, there 'tis, wheel car (car wheel)."

Age 3 years 7 months. Freda now had 671 spoken words and phrases and was heard, in the clinic, to put five words together. She had some ideas of her own as to how she wanted to play.

Guidance to her mother included demonstration of the effectiveness of simple ways of winning and keeping Freda's co-operation in play situations while using the speech trainer. Two-way verbal communication between mother and child was becoming a main factor indeed in their mutual relationship. Each could ask the other to give things and to do things. Freda had begun to understand questions and to answer them. She looked to her mother as a source of information and for suggestions as to how they should play.

A variety of grammatical parts of speech had now, for several months, occurred in Freda's spontaneous talking. While nouns predominated there were also verbs, adjectives, prepositions and adverbs. Perhaps it should be emphasised that this was entirely a product of the mother's informal and colloquial method of talking to Freda in sentences. After Freda had reached the age of four it was felt to be advisable deliberately to give emphasis to prepositions—needed for communicating the positioning of the toys— "put the horse *under* the tree, put the duck *on* the pond", etc.

Age 3 years 10 months. Auditory discrimination had now developed to the point that through the speech trainer Freda heard and repeated correctly a number of words that were said when she was not looking—chair, shoes, clock, bed, pipe. She had been found to do best when given the full power of the speech training aid—much later when she was eight years old a speech audiogram confirmed this. Amongst the longest sentences that Freda spoke in a clinic session were—"wash windows dirty clean, come on Mummy, do it". She had acquired a habit of talking to herself a great deal. We heard her say "no dollies, baby bath, oh shocking, where Doreen? no church". Her mother's list of her expressive vocabulary now included 835 words, with a wide range—"aphbet (alphabet). recor(d) p(l)ayer, swimmy-poo(l), catus (cactus), pansy, d(r)eadful, by, with, grow(l), p(r)operly, tevisha (television)", etc.

Age 4 years. Use of phrases and sentences was now a main feature of Freda's talking at home—"Daddy coming for breakfast, Freda have a swing, Doreen's gone out with George, Baby Russell sleep caricot in bedroom, Dolly broken, Daddy will mend it". One day at a guidance session Freda was working extremely well with domestic toys, which included furniture and a doll with day and night clothes. She said "dolly put on dressing gown" then she put the doll to bed and quite spontaneously recited a prayer, whispering the words. She called the dressing-gown cord a "string", pronouncing the consonant group perfectly.

Age 4 years 6 months. A transcription of 127 different words used by Freda, while talking during a guidance session, showed that she was using a good many verbs but that they were inadequate in variety. All parts of speech were represented. Many of her sentences consisted of four or five words. Sometimes they conformed to normal grammatical English—"she's got a mattress, Freda wants a big pram, show baby Nana's clock, I want a pillow". There are others which do not so conform. "Where Mummy washing sink? Baby wants sit up tea, wants see Roger's school, Where's push chair? Nana got big ticktock." In most cases the words needed to normalise a sentence seem to be the very short ones, which in ordinary colloquial speech are of very brief duration and unstressed.

It was noticed that Freda was still using present tenses when referring to past situations. Her mother was advised to pick up what she had said and repeat it but using the correct tense. To encourage a freer use of pronouns by Freda it was suggested that her mother should try games and competitions involving contrasts between pronouns, e.g. sharing out things with "one for you, one for me. I'll have that one, you have this one."

Age 5 years. Freda was now sure of the pronouns I, me and you, although still less certain of he and she, his and hers. In the clinic she talked continuously with her mother and the guider about things past, present and future. She was heard using a conditional tense, "John would never put toys on table." She very much enjoyed playing with words, e.g. calling one doll "Linda" and another "Custard!"

Some of the sentences that her mother transcribed while Freda was playing for an hour at home are as follows:

What are you talking about?
I'll be the post box, shall I?
I'm talking to Timothy 'cos he's very small.
Christine not going to my school.
She's not coming to my house, Timothy says no.
Boy get hurt, look, what a shame!
Mummy, be careful, mind you'll hurt yourself.

(Note: When Freda was 8 years 5 months old she was re-examined in the University Clinic. Her intelligence on the Wechsler Child Scale was found average—I.Q. 94. On the Peabody Picture Vocabulary Test she reached a standard normal to an average eight-year-old unhandicapped child.)

Sheila

When Sheila was only ten months old her deafness was detected through a screening test by a health visitor who reported an absolute absence of response to sound. The consultant otologist who examined her could find no probable cause for the condition either before or after birth. He referred her to the Manchester University clinic and at the initial test no responses to sound were obtained there. In spite of what was subsequently revealed as profound deafness Sheila's progress through home training was outstandingly good.

Her parents were both teachers. They had two other children, one five and the other eight, at the time of Sheila's first referral. Her mother gave up teaching for several years and both parents treated the home training as a priority. Because of a very heavy case-load at the University clinic regular parent guidance could not be begun in this case until Sheila had reached the age of 1 year 2 months, but the mother had already started to put into practice recommendations previously made to her. By the time of the second visit the parents had made a pair of ear muffs for the telephones of the speech trainer headset. She had begun to use the speech trainer at home and did so for two periods of ten minutes each in the clinic. Both father and mother were successful in interesting Sheila in suitable forms of play and Sheila had started to glance briefly at the face of a speaker.

At this stage Sheila was naturally very lively and distractable. Sometimes she would reject the speech trainer but when she wore the headset she enjoyed seeing and hearing things like a large wooden farm animal being bumped across the table. Perhaps not surprisingly, her parents were inclined to use only single words when speaking to her and had to be convinced that for them to talk in sentences was more to her advantage.

Age 1 year 5 months. By this time Sheila had made marked progress. In the clinic one day she sat and wore the headset for thirty-five minutes in a series of play situations with her mother. She had begun to use single words spontaneously although in-

13

completely, for instance "'ow (cow), pi (pig)" and tried to imitate "moo" and "quack-quack". Perhaps because of anxiety that Sheila should become as quickly as possible a talking child, her parents had to be helped to discover an informal approach. It was shown to them that by giving Sheila some of the initiative in play with them she could be stimulated to more spontaneous vocalisation and to have greater desire to communicate.

Two tape recordings of Sheila with her mother using a speech trainer illustrate at once both her progress and her difficulties. In the first recording, taken at the age of 1 year 10 months, she tries to speak spontaneously but when she does so is only able to utter vowel sounds, "'a-ou (thank you), ow-er (powder), u air (brush hair)." When her mother says "bark, bark", Sheila's imitation is "ba ba". Attempting to imitate her mother's "comb hair", she says "o air". For her mother's "kettle" she repeats "ku". When her mother speaks of a doll as wearing trousers, Sheila corrects the description to "a-ie" (panties). In the second recording at 4 years 1 month Sheila converses fluently and quickly in sentences with quite a wide range of vocabulary. Statements predominate but on occasion Sheila asks a question. Her longest sentence includes eleven words. She articulates a variety of consonants, including /s/, /j/, /br/, /pr/. There are consonantal substitutions and omissions, especially of final consonants, e.g. "Tay a home Micky Renshaw" for "Take that home to Mrs. Renshaw." "I want some mea (meat). Got to take 'e (them) home fir(st)." "I want to take the toil (soil) out", after asking for a spade. When pretending to pack a suitcase she is asked what to put in it. She replies "some tutti frutis, . . . and some pyjama and some clean so' (socks) and some choe (shoes) . . . and a clean dre' (dress)". Some of her sentences are normally or almost normally articulated but her verbalisation of her thinking does not seem typical of an un-handicapped four-year-old child, "I want some loaf of bread at loaf of bread shop." "You haven't put the packet paper" meaning "you haven't wrapped up the packet." "He want some hat and coa(t) and choes (shoes)." In the second recording her voice appears high-pitched even for a child of her own age. For a very deaf child of her age Sheila talks unusually well.

A pure-tone audiogram using the performance technique was made when Sheila was only 2 years 6 months old. It indicated very severe to profound bilateral deafness with evidence of some acuity throughout the speech range of hearing. Subsequently, during a period when she was two to three years old, some fluctuations in her hearing were diagnosed. Surgery in the form of bilateral aspirations and an adenoidectomy were found to have brought beneficial results including some increase in auditory acuity in the lower-pitched part of the speech spectrum. At the age of 2 years 4 months an electro-encephalographic record of response to sound during sleep was made in hospital. The only consistent response obtained was to very loud speech at the 110 decibel level.[1]

Beginning at the age of two years Sheila's mental growth was assessed by several different psychologists. All agreed that she was highly intelligent. When she was three years old it was stated that she had always been advanced in manipulative and imaginative play and that six months earlier she was reported to have begun to enjoy cutting out and to have shown interest in using plastic shapes to make objects. At three years of age her imaginative play was assessed as of three and a half year level. The sound recording, which we have quoted, when Sheila was four years old illustrates the mental agility with which Sheila invented dialogue in play situations.

SHORT HISTORIES

Molly
Molly's profound deafness was diagnosed as due to a not very common hereditary factor. Known as Waardenburg's Syndrome, it has been found to be associated with malformation of the inner angles of the eyelids, differently coloured eyes and a white forelock. Her mother suspected deafness when Molly's age was only nine months. At 1 year 1 month, when first seen in the Manchester University clinic, she used her voice only sometimes, relying on gesture to ask for things. She was considered, during two and a half years of home training under clinic guidance, to be normally intelligent. Her home was middle class and there was one older child. Quite early she was found to need and was supplied with a super-power aid. A speech training hearing aid, when she had become accustomed to it, helped much to stimulate her spontaneous

[1] A pure-tone audiogram, made when Sheila's age was 3 years 11 months, is included and discussed in Chapter Six.

15

use of voice. Later still in the course of research on selective prescription of hearing aids in the Manchester University Department, Molly was found to be one of those children for whom considerable amplification of all the lower-pitched part of the speech spectrum was most important.

At the beginning learning to lipread was a great help to Molly. By the age of 2 years 2 months she could discriminate fifty words or more. When asked she would point out many objects and pictures named by the speaker—some animals, a tree, the grass and house, etc. She was not yet prepared to wear the headset of the speech trainer for any length of time. Her mother needed all possible support at this period. Four months later Molly had begun to accept the speech trainer during special play sessions. She had started to vocalise more frequently than before. An attempt to say "yellow" was one of her first words. In the following months mother and child learnt to enjoy simple forms of co-operative play together. Molly attempted more words and her receptive vocabulary widened, including words like "pheasant, squirrel, sky". She began putting words together, her utterances consisting chiefly of vowels, at the age of 3 years 2 months. Seven weeks later she was heard to say, in the clinic, spontaneously but in most cases imperfectly, "bath, pram, baby in pram, cow, bull, pig, baby pig, baa lamb, milk, dog, house, horse, quack-quack". Examples of her articulation were "purp (purple), peeks (pink), geen (green)". Simple but complete sentences began to appear in Molly's spontaneous talking at about this time, e.g. "put the baby in the pram". One day in the clinic when her mother said "Daddy has gone to work in the car" Molly replied, "No, no, daddy gone to work on bus"—which was correct. Her intonation was steadily improving and consonants were more frequent—"torsher (saucer), tottoddie (crocodile), car".

By the time Molly went to a school for the deaf at the age of four she was continually using sentences. As a profoundly deaf child she needed full-time education by qualified teachers of the deaf.

Roger
Roger's educational management involved a complex of different problems. He was referred to the University clinic by a consultant paediatrician primarily because he had congenitally abnormal

ears. His age was nine months and no surgery was contemplated. This decision was repeated by a consultant otologist when Roger had reached the age of four. There was a convergent squint for which he wore spectacles for two and a half years, prescribed by a consultant ophthalmologist. These were no longer necessary after he had had an eye operation. Roger did not sit without support until he was thirteen months old. He walked unsupported four months later. Soon afterwards a greater maturation of the nervous system was diagnosed. When first seen he had responded only to very loud sound, now he was shown to hear the equivalent in loudness of a moderately loud voice at three feet—60 decibels. A pure-tone audiogram was made when he was 3 years 2 months old. It indicates clearly that Roger had a hearing potential of a kind that is usually found among children designated as partially deaf or hard of hearing. His progress was slow until he approached the age of three. He seems to have needed training to direct his attention and arouse his interest for sound. His delayed motor development, which included extremely poor manipulation, created great difficulties for his mother. The need to use large wooden toys and floor play until a later age than that of most home training children helped to complicate the use of the speech trainer. He was supplied with a bone-conduction hearing aid but to bring about use of a speech trainer was urgent.

Despite these problems by the age of 3 years 2 months Roger was understanding a great deal of what was said to him. He was talking in phrases and incomplete sentences. He obeyed commands, answered questions and understood references to past and future. Any sudden change of context still caused him difficulty and he tended to take refuge in echolalia, i.e. repeating the words that had been addressed to him. By this time establishment of spoken communication with her child had greatly lessened Roger's mother's difficulties. Before he was two years old she had made great progress. Specifically, under guidance, she had trained herself to talk with a kindly, though clear, voice and intonation and with a lively, cheerful facial expression.

A tape recording of Roger, then 4 years 4 months old, with his mother, shows him to be talking fluently and colloquially in sentences with a wide vocabulary. The situation is play with a country scene. There are little toy people and animals that can be moved about on a coloured paper base, which represents fields and a road. In answer to his mother's "Shall we have a bull?" Roger replies "Yes, to chase it," and, later on, "It's a baby cow, that one . . . Oh, it won't stand up . . . I want something else to show you . . . Oh, it goes with that brown one . . . What's that there? . . . That lady can fight." These and many other sentences are spoken very clearly. Others are indistinct. His voice seems unduly high-pitched. We would agree with the decision taken to place him in a special unit for partially-hearing children, attached to an ordinary school.

Ann

Ann presented still a different problem. A consultant otologist referred her to the Manchester University Audiology Clinic when she was 2 years 7 months old. He had found that she was apparently unable to talk but certainly heard loud sounds. She had been born at home, four weeks post-mature, with a birth-weight of 11 lbs. It was stated that she was "black when born". Her mother had suspected deafness when Ann was eighteen months old and had been very anxious to have her condition investigated but had been advised that Ann would talk when she was older. The baby was stated to have been able to sit unsupported at the age of five months and to stand unsupported at eleven months.

Tests in the University clinic confirmed that Ann could hear very loud sound—at the 80–90 decibel level—throughout at least the greater part of the range of pitch involved in speech. Her parents were responsible people—her father a foreman driver. They had two younger children. Their home training of Ann, under guidance, was very good. It was clear that the hearing aids helped but by the age of four and a half years her spoken language was less well developed than that of other deaf children reported in this chapter. Later beginning of home training, than for most of them, may well have been a factor.

When Ann was three years old a speech training aid was lent to her parents for use in short, special play sessions at home. A tape recording, made at that time, shows Ann vocalising so much that it was difficult for her mother to talk to her. It seems that this is because the child so much enjoyed hearing her own voice amplified. In personal-social development she was not backward. At 3 years 6 months she liked copying her mother drawing figures on paper and digging in the garden. She ate with knife and fork, was starting to dress herself and cleaned her own teeth.

In the clinic, between the ages of three and a half years and four years, Ann was heard using words spontaneously, e.g. exclaiming "rude" when a doll's dress was unfastened. She imitated a sequence of three words easily, although imperfectly—"o(n) the chair, that one too, that a (t)eapo(t), ashoo m' (excuse me)". She used some consonants recognisably and vowels rather more often so. At this stage her mother needed and was given renewed help in microphone techniques and use on her own part of a clear, strong voice. She was shown, also, that Ann's Medresco hearing aid that she now wore all day should be high up on her chest for her to hear better her own voice and attempts to talk. A more powerful wearable aid was not long afterwards obtained for her.

A tape recording, when Ann had reached the age of 4 years 5 months, confirmed that she was a talking child. In her spontaneous utterances she was putting words together but not often in complete sentences. Vocabulary was continuing to grow. Articulation of consonants was still a problem, e.g. "wy 'oo 'o' (white blue socks), pa' ah' (pants on)". Some of the consonants that she did use were not only labials, e.g. "Doddy (Noddy), that shair (that's a chair), more pease (more please), My'a baby doll (Michael's baby doll)". When her mother repeated some of her utterances back to her, with careful speech. through the microphone Ann's articulation was often much improved—"piano, watch, sit, chair" and "settee" were correct.

In subsequent chapters of this book we describe our current methods to ensure that children with defective hearing are found early in their lives and systematised methods of training modified for individual needs and conditions.

2
How hearing-impaired children can be found —screening tests

Screening tests have long been widely accepted and extensively used for the detection of hearing defects among infants and young children. The purpose of this chapter is to describe how we ourselves have found it possible in recent years to make our tests increasingly efficient. Already in Chapter One, case histories have been quoted that illustrate how detection of auditory impairment by screening tests often proves the first step towards making sure that children with varying degrees of deafness have the best possible opportunity of learning to talk in the critical first years of life. Also, for some children, early detection, when it leads to referral to consultant otologists, ensures the possibility of treatment that may prevent deafness from becoming permanent or else ameliorate it.

Perhaps the difference between screening and diagnostic testing still needs to be made clear. The aim of screening tests is to find children who are not responding normally to sound. Very often this is the responsibility of health visitors or other public health nurses. There can be a variety of reasons for a child's failure to respond to sound normally. For clinical diagnosis a wide range of facilities is frequently necessary and nowadays increasingly available in many countries. It is becoming more and more accepted that audiologists, otolaryngologists, paediatricians, psychologists, psychiatrists, with public health doctors and general practitioners, should provide a co-ordinated and comprehensive service. Of course, not every child who is found unable to respond normally to sound needs examination in all these directions. Diversity of problems that may occur has been emphasised by the high incidence of multiple handicaps resulting from the rubella epidemics that occurred in the Eastern States of the U.S.A. from 1964 to 1965. Our screening tests of hearing have been described as a valuable means of evaluating the very young child's relation to his environment.

Some authorities have advocated restriction of screening tests to children described as belonging to "risk groups". By these are meant children whose family or individual histories are held to indicate that they may be subject to some factor which may cause deafness. Examples are a positive family history of deafness, a virus infection such as german measles during the early months of pregnancy and infections such as meningitis and measles during early childhood. Obviously, screening in high risk cases is very important. Full weight needs to be given, however, to reports by otologists who have researched on deafness in childhood that in a large number of cases—forty per cent is common—they diagnose the cause of deafness as unknown. When conducting over many years, on behalf of public health authorities, courses of training for health visitors in making screening tests, we are accustomed to finding quite frequently children who are in fact unable to respond to sound normally although there has previously been no question of their having any hearing problem.

/ Once it is accepted, as it has been by many public health departments in the United Kingdom, that all infants and young children should be screened, training and apparatus become necessary for a very large number of workers. For children under twelve months of age the screening tests are sometimes listed in publicity about "Baby's first year engagements". There are also the children of later ages who will not have routine medical examinations until they go to school. Our tests, therefore, cover the whole age-range up to five years. Our records for 4,224 children show that a significant number have been identified for the first time as hearing impaired between the ages of one and five years. The apparatus and methodology of the tests, because of the very large scale of testing that is required, must appear to be simple. It would be impracticable to rely on electronic equipment. Nevertheless, the production of the test stimuli is technologically based.

Laboratory investigations of the sound stimuli used in our tests have been made in the Department of Audiology and Education of the Deaf, University of Manchester. Here a non-technical explanation may be of help to non-professional readers. It is of the utmost importance to verify a child's ability to hear sound over the wide range of pitch produced during the utterance of human speech. On present evidence this range varies little, if at all, in different languages. We may refer to musical standards. An adult male voice produces some sound pitched an octave or more lower than the piano middle C. At the upper end of the range is very high-pitched sound important to complete hearing of consonants that include /s/ and /th/ (think), extending to about five octaves above middle C. Of course, women's voices are almost always higher pitched than men's and children's voices higher pitched than women's. A very interesting fact, however, is that the distinguishing features of the sound patterns of particular vowels and consonants in a language vary comparatively little whether uttered by men, women or children. A psychological fact which cannot be over-emphasised is that children learning to talk for the first time need to have good hearing over the whole of the speech range—the sound patterns of vowels and consonants in their entirety. The position is quite different when older children or adults with unimpaired hearing who have been through the whole experience of speech acquisition find themselves in a situation in which they can only hear speech imperfectly. As long as we are listening to a familiar form of speech conveying fairly familiar information we can make sense of what we hear and need not be aware of any difficulty even although the sound patterns reaching our ears are, in fact, incomplete. We can manage with less than the full number of cues just because we can draw on enough memories of having heard them all. In screening tests of the hearing of infants and young children it is absolutely essential to detect any cases in which some of the auditory cues to speech are being missed.

Without screening tests a degree of deafness to high tones is by no means always detected in early childhood. It is apt to be overlooked, for instance, in a child if he hears low tones, for example the sound of a voice, across a room or even from another room. It was the subject of one of our first researches at Manchester University. We found that severe high-tone deafness when associated with much better hearing for lower tones sometimes seriously delays or even prevents speech development. Even in recent years we have met cases in which it has been mistaken for mental subnormality. In an investigation involving 24,541 school children by Erie County Health Department, Buffalo, N.Y., four per thousand were found to suffer from exclusively high-tone deafness. A much larger proportion, 3·5 per cent of the total number screened, had significant hearing impairments affecting acuity for less high-pitched sound, although sometimes high tones as well. These figures relate to children in ordinary schools. Those in special schools were not included in the survey. Compared with a control group of children, those with high-tone deafness were found to exhibit learning failure, behaviour difficulties and speech defects much more frequently. By otologists high-tone deafness is very often diagnosed as due to "perceptive deafness". This means that it is caused by a pathology of the inner ear and, therefore, unlike many middle-ear conditions impossible to ameliorate or cure by medical treatment or surgery.

Hearing for tones in the lower half of the speech-range needs also to be searchingly tested in a screening procedure. This has to be done in such a way as to ensure that no auditory impairment due to past or present middle ear trouble is overlooked. An essential skill for the tester is to produce sound stimuli at minimal intensities—minimal levels of loudness. Practice with a sound level meter is so useful in a training course and periodically afterwards.

Infants and young children, as a part of normal development, learn gradually to discriminate between different kinds of sound —different sound patterns. Of all types of sound pattern one of the earliest to be discriminated and recognised by infants is that of the human voice. Psychologists have long recognised that the human voice begins to be meaningful to a baby within a few months of birth. Most of the meanings are learnt because certain kinds of sound are usually to be heard simultaneously with certain kinds of experience through other senses. To a baby with unimpaired hearing his mother's voice becomes a signal telling him that he is about to be fed, tended and loved. She may be outside his field of vision but he learns to expect that he may soon feel the warmth of her handling. Voices become so important that by the time babies are seven months old or sometimes before that we find that they can respond to a sentence spoken in the quietest tones that testers, after training and practice, can produce. We would emphasise that the duration of the utterance is often significant to its effectiveness as a test of hearing at this stage.

The nature of a baby's behaviour when responding to sound is much further developed when through maturation as part of normal growth he becomes able freely to rotate eyes and head towards an object of interest. Ability to sit unsupported has the effect of equipping him to see much more of what is going on around him. His visible world gains larger dimensions than the one available to him while lying in a cot or pram. By the age of seven months most babies have reached both these stages of development. They are ready for our screening tests. For a period of an infant's life which does not seem to have been assessed, perhaps lasting noticeably for about eighteen months, he passes through a phase of very frequently looking to see "What made that sound?" This key fact that certain kinds of faint sound in certain conditions stimulate babies to rotate eyes and head to look straight at a source of sound is the basis upon which we train workers making screening tests to recognise whether a response is decisive. In the absence of much training and experience in this special field reliance on less easily identifiable behaviour on the part of a child can make for unreliability in testing.

Of course, babies learn to recognise as meaningful to themselves other sounds, besides that of the human voice. Many of them turn quickly to the noise made by stirring a cup with a spoon. Some years before writing this book we discontinued that as an item in our tests because laboratory analysis showed that the sound produced in that way begins with an impact noise too loud for our purpose. It also covers too wide a range of pitch which again is the reason why we disregarded an item that involved the rustling of tissue paper. On the other hand very high-pitched rattles, as calibrated in the Manchester University Department's laboratories, when used with the special movement described below, provide a source of extremely faint sound limited to a narrow range of very high pitch. Perhaps it needs to be emphasised that tests with sounds of greater than minimal loudness risk failure to detect hearing impairment that in the long view may be important. This, of course, is the objection to use of any test stimulus, when screening, loud enough to evoke a startle response.

We have come to recognise that, whenever it is at all possible, screening tests of infants should be made by two trained workers. This is because of great variations that can occur at any one time in a particular child's state of attention. As the famous child psychologist, Jean Piaget, has stated, a baby whose attention is directed to playing with his feet or any form of tactile sensation is not very likely to take notice of slighter stimulation through his distance sense of hearing. In routine infant welfare work it may be unavoidable to make a screening test of a baby at a time when he is accustomed to sleep or is suffering discomfort while teething. It is to cope with possible distractions of these kinds, expected or unexpected, that a second trained worker is invaluable. For want of a better word we refer to the second worker as the "occupier".

Tester and occupier achieve far the best results when accustomed to work together with particular attention to the timing of their actions. When screening infants in the seven to eighteen months' age range the occupier acts first. She chooses some toys the sight of which, when moved about in a lively manner, are likely to interest the infant who is to be tested. When a health centre is the venue for testing the occupier takes one of them, say a brightly coloured teddy bear, to the waiting room. She does her best to attract the child's interest in it, talking about it at the same time with a cheerful voice. She directs the child's attention in this way while accompanying mother and child to the testing room. Then mother, with child on her knees, and occupier sit down facing each other across a small table. The occupier makes sure that the mother seats the child facing squarely towards her.

To ensure that the child does not fail in the screening test through any physical disability that can hinder free rotation of the head, or that head control is not affected by delay in maturation, the occupier moves an attractive toy slowly, first to one side and then to the other. The toy needs to be moved far enough to stimulate the child to turn his head from facing forward, through an angle of 90 degrees, to each side. In this and always when seeking to hold an infant's attention an occupier needs to watch carefully the movements of the infant's eyes and to make sure that she manipulates a toy in such a way as to cause the infant to focus visually on it. Accompanying all her movements of toys she finds it very helpful to talk about them with a clear and cheerful voice. "Hush-hush" voices are to be avoided. It is also better not to keep addressing the child by name. It is to the toy that the occupier seeks to attract the child's attenion, not to herself. Only one toy should be in use or visible at any one time. Before bringing mother and infant into the clinic the occupier hides some alternative toys under the table or under her chair. It is best to avoid frequent changes of toys and only to make a change in the event of seeming to lose a child's interest. Unusual ways of manipulating toys pay off well. Teddy can be tossed upwards and caught again, the occupier saying "Up he goes" each time that she does this. He can be swung by his ears. A large bright coloured ball can be bounced on the table while the occupier says "Bump, bump, bump!" or it can be made to spin. It can be rolled up over one's face and over one's head to disappear behind it. This last has the advantage of attracting the infant to look straight forward and upward.

While this stimulation and alerting of the child's attention is in progress the tester takes position to right or left of him, very quietly, in such a way that the child remains unaware of her movements. It is to contribute to this extreme quietness of movement that some form of soft floor covering is useful. No one else but the occupier should be within the child's field of vision, nor should the child be able to see any toys in the room or be distracted by movements outside a window.

The direction with regard to the child's ears from which the test stimuli are produced is important. An infant is most effectively stimulated to localise a source of sound, quickly and accurately, by focusing his eyes on it when the sound is made at the same height from the floor as his right or left ear and exactly opposite to it. To achieve this when uttering the sentence (Item Sp. 1 in the schedule) the tester needs to bend forward and downwards so that his mouth is on a level with the child's ear. Similarly, using a test rattle, the tester needs to hold it in front of her in the required position. This eliminates any possibility that the child may catch sight of her body. We have found with infants seven to eighteen months that the most suitable distance from the ear at which to produce the sound stimuli is 1 metre (3–4 feet).

Very careful timing of the test sounds is equally important. The optimum moment is always when the occupier has alerted the child but has suddenly caused the toy to disappear and has herself become silent. What is wanted is that at this very moment the child should be free to attend to stimulation from a different source. The occupier looks downwards. She takes care not to look into the child's eyes and, of course, not in the direction of the tester. Close collaboration between the two workers is necessary. If the child responds decisively to a test sound the occupier first allows him time to see what made that noise. Then she resumes her part. Should the child fail to respond the occupying is resumed at once.

CHILDREN AGED ABOUT SEVEN TO EIGHTEEN MONTHS

In detail, methods by which the tester produces the sound stimuli for infants aged about seven to eighteen months are as follows. In our schedule items using voice and words are referred to by the abbreviation "Sp.". All others, essentially tests of auditory acuity, are given the abbreviation "A".

Item 1 (Sp. 1). Eight syllable sentence

For a normally developing infant this is largely a test, as we have suggested earlier, to find whether he can hear human speech faintly uttered. It is likely that the factor of voice having become significant to him enters into the picture whether or not he has got as far as to understand much of what is said. Sentences suitable for this item may include "Look what a lovely toy I've got here", "Oh look, I've come over here now". It will be noticed that words in which /s/ occurs are excluded. This is to avoid a possibility that a child, suffering from an aural condition that leaves unaffected acuity for very high tones but involves deafness for sound in other parts of the speech range of pitch, can appear to respond to a sentence when in fact he has only heard the sibilant /s/. Some infants turn as soon as a sentence begins to be uttered. Others need sound of longer duration. Hence our stipulation that the sentence used should include eight syllables. Hurried speech is to be avoided. The sentence needs to be spoken, not whispered. The sound patterning of whispered speech is much different from that which is spoken with the voice. To achieve minimal intensity in utterance of a test sentence workers seem to find it helpful to use the lowest pitched

27

tones of voice that they can produce in a natural manner. Apparently this assists them in relaxing the muscular systems that are involved.

Item 2 (A.1). High rattle

In our tests the selected and calibrated rattles are manipulated in a special way. They are not shaken at all in the way that is usual with rattles. Holding its long handle between thumb and first finger the tester, when the right moment arrives, slightly rotates the rattle. This causes the tiny pellets to rub frictionally against the inside of the case at a very low level of intensity. In a screening test it is essential not to increase the loudness of the sound because a child fails to respond. Often it is enough for the tester to change the direction from which the sound is reaching a child—from the right side to the left or vice versa. Allowance has to be made for children all of whose responses during screening are seen to be slow. For them the duration of the sound that the tester makes with the rattle has to be prolonged. A further step with a child unresponsive to the high rattle is for the occupier to use a duplicate of it instead of a toy. She interests the child simultaneously in watching the movements that she makes with it, as an attractive bright object, and in hearing the sound that she makes by shaking it rather noisily. Just as with the toys that she uses, she makes the rattle disappear. Instantly the tester, from one side of the child or the other, uses her rattle to produce the standard A.1 stimulus. As a result of this method many children who appear otherwise unable to hear the sound are led to respond quickly and decisively. It is as well for the child not to see that there are two rattles.

Item 3 (A.2). "Boo-oo-oo-oo-oo"

The sound stimulus represented by this item has been chosen especially to test the acuity of infants for low-pitched sound. Laboratory analysis shows the vowel /oo/ to have the greater part of its sound energy within a range of pitch lower than many other vowels and most consonants. This item A.2 not only concentrates on testing acuity for lower tones to an extent that is not possible with Sp.1, there is also the practical point that this sound stimulus is given sufficient duration to cater for those children who tend always to be rather slow in responding. Most of us need practice to produce an /oo/ sound at truly minimal intensity. As in utterance of the Sp.1 sentence, it is necessary to pitch one's voice low. We have found that many workers are helped to achieve the essential degree of relaxation by beginning the sound stimulus with a consonant /b/ very quietly uttered. To make this item interesting and attention-catching to most infants the /oo/ syllables have to be uttered rhythmically but with only the least possible variation of their loudness or pitch. Clinically, this item is useful for screening out those infants with hearing impairments for low tones that are later diagnosed as associated with infections of the middle ear. It is not uncommon in cases of this kind to find that acuity for high tones is not affected. Earlier versions of our schedule included use of a specially selected rattle in place of the current item. The main feature of its construction was a fairly large single ball within a cylindrical case. Supplies are no longer available.

Item 4 (A.3). "S-s-s-s ——"
/S/ is the highest pitched consonant that it is practicable to employ as a screening test of hearing for high tones. Acuity in the relevant range of pitch is so important to a child that with the high rattle item it forms a double check of this. Owing to the fact that it is made in a different way it is a precaution against any unintentional misuse of the high rattle. We recommend that to have passed the whole screening test satisfactorily an infant should be found to have made a normal response both to the high rattle and to the /s/.

Normal articulation is necessary. Here again some workers find themselves to need practice, with expert help, to become able to articulate a pure /s/ when this consonant is separated from any word. Also, quite distinctively, and to attract quick attention from many infants, a series of /s/ sounds has to be repeated with a noticeable rhythm. When uttered rhythmically the sound suggests something moving, something happening. This A.4 item can readily be produced at a low intensity appropriate to screening.

In what order is it best for the tester to present the sound stimuli? On the whole it has proved most effective to begin with item Sp. 1—the sentence. This is perhaps because it is associated with the kind of sound that is likely to have become most meaningful to a baby.

Once testing has begun there are two practical considerations. First, that we have observed that the attention of most infants tends to be attracted quickly to a sound when it contrasts in quality with a previous one to which they have just responded. Second, that to reduce a risk of causing undesired noises—and for other reasons—the tester should move about as little as possible.

The order of items which we prefer is as follows:

Right side	Sp.1 sentence, then A.1 high rattle.
Left side	Ditto.
Left side	A.2 "Boo-Ooo-Ooo-Ooo" (or low rattle), then A.3 "S-S-S-S".
Right side	Ditto.

Inevitably, this order has sometimes to be varied with a child who fails to respond to one or more items after one or two presentations. As a rule it is useful in such cases to change to a contrasting stimulus and to return later to the previous item.

CHILDREN AGED ABOUT 19 TO 33 MONTHS

Item 5 (Sp.2). Small toy test
The main purpose of this item is to screen out children who present one or other or both of two kinds of difficulty. There are those whose auditory acuity is impaired. Others have difficulty in understanding what is said although not suffering from deafness in the usual sense of that word. Some causes of deafness impair both auditory acuity and auditory discrimination. Children in all three groups require to be found and referred for diagnostic testing and examination.

The essence of the method of Item Sp.2 is that the tester wins the co-operation of the child in a simple form of play. It is natural for children in this age group to enjoy putting one thing into another.

Two categories of toys are used. There are those employed as receptacles—these may include a pram, a bath, a bed, a boat, a chair. Then there are objects that a child in the age range is normally able to recognise and put into one of the receptacles, such as a baby or tiny doll, a dog, a cat, a tiny teddy bear. Both receptacles and objects to put in them have to be small enough for a little group of them to be on the table at one and the same time and within easy reach of a very young child.

The tester begins by going to the waiting room with one of the most brightly coloured receptacles, straightaway to win and hold the child's interest. Back in the clinic the child is seated on a nursery school type of low chair at a low table with mother sitting beside him. Putting the toy on the table immediately in front of the child the tester quickly produces another toy to put into it. Speaking in natural, very friendly tones she asks the child to put the object into the receptacle—e.g. "Put the baby in the pram." It is better for her not to carry out the act herself. It is essential for the child to begin and to keep doing what is asked. Quite often a child will put the baby in the pram before he is asked to do so which is surely some evidence of his natural re-action to the situation. Next, the tester produces from a source, that she needs to keep hidden but close at hand, a second receptacle. She asks the child to move the object from the first receptacle into it saying "Put the —— into the ——." A third receptacle is placed in front of the child and he is asked to move the object into it. Three receptacles on the table are enough. Now a second object is introduced, e.g. the dog. The child is asked to put it into one of the receptacles.

Now, without any break, the test proper begins. Gradually the tester reduces the loudness of her voice. Simultaneously she increases the distance between herself and the child to about one and a half metres or four to five feet. By her requests to the child she keeps the toys on the move. Occasionally by having two objects put into a single receptacle she increases the total number of different moves that can be made, with the result that the test of the child's auditory discrimination becomes more searching. A child with unimpaired hearing should be able to respond correctly to at least two or three requests uttered at a minimal level of loudness from either side of him.

The preparatory stage of making sure whether or not the child can understand requests put with normal loudness of voice is very important. To screen out children with partial impair-ments of hearing reduction of loudness has to be made skilfully.

Here, as in Item Sp.1, whispered speech is to be avoided. Testers need to practise themselves in uttering requests to children to move the toys with normal voice but at minimal loudness.

When making the requests to the children it is advisable to use deliberate and unhurried speech without, of course, breaking the sentences up into separate words. The succession of requests needs to be carefully timed. On the one hand, the child has to be allowed time to complete performance of what he has just been asked to do before a further request is made to him. On the other hand a child's co-operation needs to be continuously maintained by the tester. There should be no intervals, however brief, during which a child is left unoccupied with a risk that he may take to play on his own with the toys.

After completing the Item Sp.2 the tester says something like this—"Here's a lady with a nice ball. She's coming to play with you." The occupier quickly moves in, having previously gathered the toys that she has decided to use. Simultaneously the tester removes the Sp.2 toys. The scene is thus set for the child to be given the test of acuity for the hearing of very high pitched sound by use of the items involving the high rattle and the consonant /s/, following the same procedure as with infants aged seven to eighteen months.

CHILDREN AGED ABOUT THIRTY-FOUR MONTHS TO FIVE YEARS

Item 6 (Sp. 3). Picture book test
The objective of this item is to test children's hearing and understanding of spoken language, using a wider vocabulary than that which can be related to the Sp.2 Small Toy Test. The type of book that is required contains naturalistic pictures, brightly coloured, of daily-life situations which can be described in language normally within the vocabulary understood by children of this age range. It is important that each picture shows much detail. A good example is a picture of a boy and a girl helping their father to clean a car. Both children have dusters and are wearing wellington boots. The girl is standing on a box to reach well up one of the car's windows. There is a coloured bucket of water and some soap on the ground. All details of the car's exterior and the children's clothes are clearly portrayed. The father

is smoking a pipe. In the background is the house with its windows and roof.

Our method of using such a picture is for the tester to attract the child's interest in it by herself talking about what it shows to be going on, e.g. "Look, this boy and girl are helping their daddy to clean the car. I can see a bucket of water (pointing to it). I can see the boy's red cap (pointing to that)." As soon as she is reasonably confident that the child is interested the tester begins to involve him more actively, e.g. "I can see the car wheels. You point to them." So far the tester has spoken in normal cheerful tones, close to the child. She continues in the same way to ask the child to point to different details in the picture but only just long enough to ensure that she has the child's co-operation. As soon as this has been achieved she moves back, still asking the child to point to different things, but speaking more and more quietly. Her aim is to find whether or not the child is able to hear and understand at least three requests spoken at a minimal level of loudness from a distance of one and a half metres or five feet. The test is made first on one side and then on the other.

When leading up to the actual test the tester avoids naming or describing all the items in the picture. This is so that, when she reaches the minimal loudness level, she has some items available to which she has not previously referred when speaking more loudly. Too easy and obvious requests like "Point to the boy" (or the girl, man or car) are to be avoided. Examples of appropriate sentences are "Point to the boy's wellington boots; point to the little girl's yellow jumper; point to the man's pipe."

Testers are advised to select their own pictures to meet the requirements that we have stipulated, especially as regards range of vocabulary that is relevant. Complete familiarity with the contents of each picture and skill in exploiting them is necessary.

Children who appear at first unco-operative in this test situation can often be led to perform and enjoy it by skilful use of mummy's help. On occasion it is a good idea to ask a mother to hold her child's hand over a picture so that he has only to flex a finger to point to a named object. Sometimes children can be encouraged at the outset by mother actually "helping" him to put his finger on the object. After a very few repetitions of this method most children, who were at first unwilling or insecure,

33

co-operate happily. With all such children pictures need to be very close to them and sometimes tipped up towards them by mother.

In our experience care has to be taken to avoid a situation in which a child turns to watch the face of a tester whenever she speaks quietly to him from any distance away. The likelihood of this is increased if the tester makes use of his name to introduce her requests. Since it is not at all unusual for children who have a hearing impairment to have a habit of watching faces, to lip-read, a tester who allows this may easily be led to overlook a hearing defect. A further point is that these screening tests of underfives, if carried out correctly, often lead to detection of a monaural impairment. The possibilities of such important detection are greatly reduced when a child's head is turned towards the tester. If that happens the sound stimulus will reach both the child's ears simultaneously and with equal loudness.

Item 7 (A.4). Performance test
Normally this follows the Sp.3 Picture Test, at the conclusion of which the tester says to the child "Now we are going to play another game and this lady is coming to play with us." The occupier brings with her a box of lock bricks—preferably the round variety which are more easily fitted together by a young child than the square kind. The occupier puts all the bricks on the table near the child, talking about them as she does so. Then the tester says "See what the lady does" and turning to the occupier, speaking normally and vivaciously, tells her to "Put one on." The occupier does this in a brisk and lively fashion. She begins to build a tower. After two repetitions of this demonstration the tester, turning to the child, says "You can do that, it's easy." Beginning by speaking moderately quietly the tester progressively reduces the loudness of her voice to a just audible level, and moving gradually to a distance of one and a half metres or five feet to one side of the child. She tests the child from both right and left side in this way.

The above procedure provides a further check in cases of doubt as to whether a child has a hearing impairment. As compared with the Sp.3 Picture Test it does not, of course, evaluate a child's auditory discrimination and understanding of vocabulary. Carefully administered, however, it is a searching test of the minimal level of loudness at which speech is just audible to a child.

However, the principal use of the first part of Item 7 (A.4) is to prepare the children for a performance test in which they require to respond to a non-verbal signal. This consists of the consonant /s/ as a means of detecting hearing impairments for high tones.

After completing the first part of the test, using the "Put one on" sentence, the tester says to the child, "Now we're going to play another little game." "See what the lady does when I make a funny noise." She then utters a rather loud and exaggerated sound "S-S", on hearing which the occupier begins another tower. After two more repetitions of this demonstration—the occupier adding another brick to the tower in response to each signal—the tester says to the child "You can do that. It's easy." Then beginning by uttering "S-S" rather loudly the tester progressively reduces the loudness to a minimal level at the same time increasing her distance from the child's ear to one and a half metres or five feet. As with other items she makes the test from both right and left sides. Unimpaired hearing for /s/ is proved when a child is able to add a brick to the tower each time he hears the "S-S" signal at all the levels of loudness that are used, especially at the minimal which is essential.

The timing of the test signals "Put one on" and "S-S" is of vital importance. Short pauses between repetitions of the signals have to vary in duration. The tester needs above all to make sure that, each time, the child is waiting to hear the signal, not anticipating it. The risk of invalidating the test by anything like a rhythmic or even timing is easily demonstrated. Children are quick to pick up a rhythm and will keep adding bricks to the tower in that rhythm even if the tester become silent. If this anticipation of signals by the child occurs it is useful for the occupier to say to him, returning the brick as she does so, "O-oh, wait till you hear it."

Some children hesitate to co-operate at the beginning of the test with the "S-S" signal, probably through a feeling of uncertainty. A method that has frequently proved successful in such cases is for the occupier to say to the child "Let's do this together." She places the child's hand on a brick then, when the signal comes, she lifts the child's hand and brick with one of her own hands so that the brick is added to the tower. It is usual to find that after about three repetitions of this method the child himself, without further help, will continue to respond to the sound signals.

As a general rule it is advisable that a child who has failed to respond normally to a screening test should be given one further retest. If a second failure results referral for diagnostic examination is indicated, at an audiology clinic where available. Protracted deferment of a second test or a number of repeated retests carry a risk of delay in initiation of medical or educational treatment or both, sometimes with serious permanent consequences. It is usual for health visitors or public health nurses to take a child's history if he fails in a screening test. On occasion, e.g. if there is active otorrhoea, immediate referral for examination and diagnosis may be essential after a single test.

After our courses of training in screening tests of the hearing of children under five years health visitors are asked to send us results obtained with four children in each of the three age groups to which we have referred. We have studied reports returned by 352 health visitors on 4,224 children in 1966, 1967 and 1968. The proportion of children per age group found not to respond normally at first screening is:

Age 7–18 months	8.6 per cent
Age 19–33 months	6.5 per cent
Age 34–59 months	6.6 per cent

Our figures cover a wide range of counties from the West Riding of Yorkshire to Cheshire and North Wales and from East Anglia to Somerset. Differences in incidence of failures are surprisingly small and so are those between urban and rural areas.

In an earlier review of 1,485 children tested we found that forty-six or 3.1 per cent had been referred for audiological and otological examination. In addition there were ninety-four children or 6.3 per cent whose cases were under consideration.

It seems clear from statistics available to us that increased emphasis on "occupying" children during our screening tests, supplemented by practice with sound-level meters during courses of training for health visitors, to help them realise minimal loudness levels, has improved the reliability of initial testing. Fewer children with impairments are likely to be missed. The number of children failed at a first test but found to hear normally on retest is reduced.

Readers will have noted that the number of children that we quote as not having responded normally to sound when first tested by health visitors is largest in the age range 7–18 months. It may be relevant to quote a statement by Dr. Janet B. Hardy of the Johns Hopkins School of Medicine, Baltimore, in 1964, "The Ewing test for children from 8–14 months has proved very effective and useful, particularly in regard to respiratory problems." We ourselves, over many years, have noted that during teething a significant minority of babies fail to respond normally to our tests of their hearing. From records of follow-ups in such cases it would appear that most of those babies, but not all, regain normal hearing. We are referring, of course, when mentioning the failures, to babies who when tested were efficiently and effectively occupied.

There are other conditions reported by authorities in this field in which infants are at first found not normally responsive to sound but later can be proved to have normal hearing. These include abnormally slow maturation or development in early weeks or months with more rapid maturation later, so that the children, as it were, catch up. References are also made to infants who are not given normal experience. For instance their parents do not talk to them to the extent that is usual or they are left alone far too much.

Once more, perhaps, we should emphasise that screening is not diagnosis. Our tests, besides identifying children with defective hearing or auditory disorders, find those who are not responding normally to sound for other reasons. Our experience is that it is of great importance that all the children under both of these heads be given expert audiological testing and appropriate medical examination. We have always found that it is better for "doubtful" cases to be referred for these purposes. In 1963-64 the medical officers of the City of Manchester Health Department referred to our University Clinic 2·3 per cent of 3,638 children under five years of age who had failed an initial

SCREENING TESTS OF HEARING: UNDER-FIVES

NAME OF CHILD: _____   DATE OF BIRTH: _____

ADDRESS: _____

TESTED AT: _____CLINIC/HOME.   DATE: _____

GENERAL PRACTITIONER: Dr. _____

	TESTS USED	RESPONSE (Delete inappropriate words)	
		RIGHT EAR	LEFT EAR
AGE 7–18 months			
1. (Sp. 1)	Eight syllable sentence	Pass/Fail	Pass/Fail
2. (A.1)	High rattle	Pass/Fail	Pass/Fail
3. (A.2)	"Boo-ooo-ooo-ooo" or low rattle	Pass/Fail	Pass/Fail
4. (A.3)	"S-S-S-S . . ."	Pass/Fail	Pass/Fail
AGE 19–33 months			
5. (Sp. 2)	Small toy test	Pass/Fail	Pass/Fail
2. (A.1)	High rattle	Pass/Fail	Pass/Fail
4. (A.3)	"S-S-S-S . . ."	Pass/Fail	Pass/Fail
AGE 34 months–5 years			
6. (Sp. 3)	Picture book test	Pass/Fail	Pass/Fail
7. (A.4)	Performance "Put one on"	Pass/Fail	Pass/Fail
	followed by performance "S-S-S-S . . ."	Pass/Fail	Pass/Fail

ACTION (Tick if appropriate)

Passed. Responded normally to tests for own age-group: no further action

Failed to respond (*or* co-operate) in Tests _____ appropriate to own age-group, although PASSED Tests for a lower age group. Keep under observation and retest in _____ weeks.

Failed to respond to tests at minimal loudness, right ear *or* left ear *or* both ears: Retest within maximum period of _____ weeks.

Remarks: _____

TESTER'S SIGNATURE: _____   ASSISTED BY: _____

RETEST RESULTS AND ACTION (Tick if appropriate)   DATE: _____

(1) Passed on retest—No further action.

(2) Failed on retest: (a) Advised medical examination.

(b) Refer to Audiology Clinic.

(c) Obtained medical and developmental history as follows:

Signed: _____

screening test and also a repeat test by senior and very experienced health visitors. One-quarter of the referrals were found, in the University Audiology Clinic, to have no problem. It was accepted by all those responsible that all the referrals were very much worthwhile.

3

Different children:
different methods

Among inescapable conclusions, to which our very many years of teaching and research have led us, is one that methods of training and teaching have to be modified to suit great differences among hearing-impaired children and also among their parents.

There are great differences in development and behaviour, within particular ranges of age, among children who are considered to be unhandicapped. We have seen a very few children who were putting words together at an age of about twelve months, far more, of course, not till after the age of two. Among leading American and British authorities on the stages in which normal children learn to talk there is fairly close agreement that by the age of fifteen months the average infant can be heard to use four, five or six different words with meaning and recognisable articulation. Use of one or two words is stated to occur from the age of six to seven months, e.g. "one word apart from MAMA, DADDA". By the age of twenty-one months average American and English children have been stated as putting two words together, e.g. MILK GONE. By eighteen to twenty-one months, average unhandicapped children have been found able to carry out two or three instructions, e.g. TAKE THE BALL TO MUMMY or GO AND GET YOUR HAT. Our experience has shown how widely unhandicapped children of the present day vary on either side of these three main norms. But it is usual for all of them to pass through these successive stages and others to which we have not referred. Children with hearing problems who have to be helped to learn to talk tend to follow the same pattern—but at later ages. Methods of help and training have to take account of the needs of individual children, at whatever stage they have reached. This applies especially to children whose hearing becomes impaired or even altogether lost after they have begun to talk, following severe illness such as acute meningitis. For pre-school aged children in this category the necessities are immediate detection of deafness, immediate steps to conserve what they have already gained and skilled training to help them to progress further from whatever stage they reached previous to the onset of their deafness.

Needless to say, the great variations in the chronological ages of pre-school children requiring training because of hearing defects calls for much adaptation of methods. Referring to our personal records, we find that the youngest child whose parents brought him for guidance about home training in the Manchester University Audiology Clinic was six months old. (Much younger infants were referred for tests of hearing.) Others were first referred for guidance at different ages up to that of five years, although there was a marked increase of infants under two years after screening tests were more widely adopted.

A further set of causes for varying methods of training hearing-impaired children is variations in their ability to sit, walk, handle and manipulate objects. There is a wide range of problems under this head. We have observed at what different ages, both lower and greater than average, children believed to be unhandicapped become able to sit unsupported, to stand alone without support and to walk without help. The average age at which they can be left sitting on the floor, without support, has been quoted as nine months, standing alone at thirteen months and walking alone at fourteen to fifteen months. The same or even wider variations in motor development are found among that very complex group of children often described as having defective hearing. From this it will be seen that with some children training, at home at any rate, has to be begun while they are lying in a pram, or cot or on the floor; for others a baby's high chair, giving all round support, is very useful. Some can sit comfortably without support on a low nursery type chair at a correspondingly low table.

Very relevant to training methods is the extent to which a child has become able to manipulate objects with his hands. Dr. Ruth Griffiths, after her tests of a representative sample of 604 London babies aged between two weeks and two years, states that

the *average* eighteen-month-old infant brings objects construc-
tively into relation with one another. Her examples include ...
"he may set the doll on the chair or on the box, or the horse on
the lid, he may push the car inside as into a garage, etc." We see
children believed to be unhandicapped whose skill in handling
small objects, as evidenced in our Sp. 2, Small Toy Test, varies a
good deal on either side of this norm.

Relationships between parents and children are a key factor
in home training of hearing-impaired children. Here again it is
well to remember that problems are found in homes in which
there is no handicapped child. The added difficulty of defective
hearing can either aggravate such problems or indeed create
them because of difficulty of communication. Differences in personality and social behaviour of both parents and children are
involved. Amongst all children there are some too "shy" and
withdrawn, others by contrast friendly, outgoing and readily
co-operative. Some are fearful and anxious in any unfamiliar
situation, others secure and confident.

Parents, too, vary. Some are naturally patient and painstaking.
Others can be helped to achieve these qualities, so important to
the home training of hearing-impaired children. Some are accustomed to be chatty and talkative, others will say they have had
to learn to talk more for the sake of a deaf child. Some find it
much less difficult than others to accept a handicap in a child.
As regards a child's handicap mutual understanding, support
and co-operation between husband and wife are invaluable.

Considering children who have been found to have a hearing
problem, there are variations of special kinds to meet which
considerable adaptations of method are required. Among a
majority of them some degree of deafness has been diagnosed as
being without any complication due to an associated additional
form of handicap. With those in this category there is the first
question as to how far different kinds of sound are audible to
them or can be made audible. Differences in loudness, that are
ordinarily unnoticed by a person with normal hearing, can be
critical to the children. In Chapter Two, when describing our
screening tests for underfives we have explained how hearing for
sound of very high as well as of low pitch is necessary to complete
hearing for speech. It matters very much to the infant, when
first learning to talk. For some hard of hearing children what

they hear with the unaided ear at, say, a distance of two metres (about six feet) is very incomplete contrasted with what they hear of someone talking at the same conversational level of loudness at, say, half a metre (about twenty inches). This is partly because so many of the consonant sounds in spoken languages, e.g. /s/, are both higher in pitch than the vowel sounds and weaker in loudness. Parents of deaf infants have to take account of this. Hearing aids and microphone techniques which parents need to employ are the subject of Chapter Six. To speak to a hard of hearing child behind his back always risks preventing him from hearing as well as he can.

There are some children who, unfortunately, are very deaf but, nevertheless, can learn to hear speech distinctly with the right hearing aid used in the right way in quiet conditions. Some of the very severely deaf children, with the hearing aid selected as best for them, can hear speech usefully but imperfectly if spoken at a suitable level of loudness but not at all far from the microphone. Tests have shown that someone talking two or three metres (six or seven feet) away from the microphone may be completely inaudible. It is essential that parents, because of all the differences that can be involved, be given clear demonstrations as well as explanations as to just how to make best use of their own child's hearing.

There is another category of hearing-impaired children about whom their parents and teachers need to have as accurate knowledge as possible. Reference to it has been made in Chapter Two. This category was first identified in one of our earliest researches at Manchester University. The condition has been described as high-tone or high-frequency deafness. Some of the children in this category can hear low-pitched sound fairly normally or even, in some cases, quite normally. The low-pitched part of the sound of a conversational voice may prove to be audible across any ordinary room or from a greater distance. But because the sound-patterns of most consonants and vowels are distinguishable in terms of higher-pitched components children with this type of deafness have difficulty in discriminating words and sentences according to its degree and severity. Their capacity to benefit from hearing aids is also involved. In some of the worst cases, what a child hears resembles what is heard by a person without any hearing impairment, when listening to someone talking not at all loudly, in an adjoining room with the connecting door closed. The rise and fall of the speaker's voice and the duration of the sentences—both of them important features of speech—may be quite reasonably audible. This sort of acoustic situation is one in which a child only beginning to talk for the first time is at an enormous disadvantage as contrasted with a hearing-experienced adult. Provided that he is familiar with the language, its sound patterns and the subject that is being talked about, the adult can make do with a considerably reduced number of cues imperfectly heard. Many high-tone deaf children cannot be enabled to hear the high-pitched components of speech sound patterns by means of any form of sound amplification. The sound of /s/, for instance, in its pure and normal pattern, can never be made adequately audible, as yet, to a majority of children in the category we are discussing. Yet most of them can be *taught* to speak very well. As regards methods of training and teaching them there are two essentials. First is to ensure that there are daily and appreciable periods of time during which the sound patterns of speech reaching their ears are the best that can be contrived for them. Secondly to compensate through vision and other means for the sound cues that they never hear. How far responsibilities for these matters can be taken up by expertly guided parents and how far they can only be assumed by qualified teachers needs to be discussed later, with all the relevant details.

Only too often we have found that children who suffer from high-tone deafness that has never been detected or diagnosed are misunderstood by their own parents. "He can hear when he wants to" a father or mother may say. The background to this, of course, is that the child in question, in a situation in which the voice is loud enough to be heard by him and one in which from past experience and the set-up at the moment he gets enough cues, responds to what has been said, apparently normally. On other occasions even if he can hear the voice he just simply does not get enough cues. A very important feature of such a child's problem is that words and sentences vary greatly in the extent to which high-pitched components provide important cues to discrimination of their sound patterns. Contrast, for instance, "Go and get your coat" with "Fetch your socks", or "We are going out for a walk" with "See if there are any biscuits in the tin". To a child with high-tone deafness the consonant sounds /s/, /f/, and not infrequently /t/ are imperfectly audible and vowel sounds like /i/ in TIN less distinct than /o/ in COAT, or the /aw/ vowel in WALK.

Once we begin to analyse the capacity of hard of hearing children to identify cues audible and recognisable to them, in everyday language, it becomes all too clear that for many of them there are gaps and uncertainties as in the examples just quoted. Dr. Klockoff has reported that nearly two per cent of Swedish children have perceptive deafness. ("Perceptive" in medical diagnosis refers to deafness other than that directly caused by middle-ear infections.) He makes the point that the children's perceptive deafness varies greatly in types and degree. As is widely known, it may take the form of high-tone deafness. Some children, like some adults, have a kind of deafness that results in "recruitment". When recruitment is present, sound, to be heard at all, has to be a good deal louder than it would need to be for children or adults whose hearing is unimpaired. Then if the sound is made louder still, sometimes not very much louder, it becomes too loud in the case of speech for it to be heard as distinctly as when it is less loud. Dr. B. B. Harold, in a Manchester University research, found recruitment among children with defective hearing. Methods of using hearing aids are very much involved. As soon as the condition is identified in a child a need at once exists to find and provide conditions in which, as often as possible, he is given opportunities to hear the sound of speech evenly produced, at the level of loudness that suits him best. We mention the fact of recruitment here, although with children under five there is no simple way of identifying the condition. When perceptive deafness has been diagnosed in a very young child its possibility has to be borne in mind and careful observation continued, perhaps for a long period. As a young child's discrimination for speech develops we carefully explore the level of loudness at which he seems to hear most accurately. With older children, especially among the hard of hearing, speech audiometry, with word lists at different loudness levels, can give clear indications.

To some appreciable extent selective prescription of hearing aids has proved beneficial for children with different types of perceptive deafness. For instance, Dr. A. M. Boothroyd, when on

45

the staff of Manchester University, in his study of children with defective hearing found that some of those with high-tone deafness could hear best with hearing aids giving more amplification of the lower-pitched sound in speech than is usual.

Just as in television or radio transmissions the whole subject of background noise is very important indeed. One way in which those of us with unimpaired hearing can learn to understand this is by listening to tape recordings of speech made through a hearing aid, in an ordinarily reverberant room, with an ordinary amount of noise present. Some outside broadcasts made in very noisy out-of-door traffic conditions are an even better illustration. Our difficulty is increased if we are listening to someone talking in a way to which we are not accustomed. We can best follow such speakers if they are broadcasting from a silent studio with its sound-treated walls and other surfaces. The implication for young hearing-impaired children whether at home or, say, in playgroups is clear enough. In proportion as the loudness level of background noise approaches the loudness level of the speech which we want them to be able to hear, its audibility and distinctness—the number of cues made available to them—are sharply reduced. Organisation and methods of training have to be planned to compensate.

The extent to which deafness amongst very young children eliminates the possibility of their hearing very quiet sound, or perhaps moderately loud sound, or even quite loud sound, is not often difficult to measure. Modern techniques of testing, for instance by free-field audiometers replacing pitch pipes with special skills in child handling, have seen to that.

The extent to which a young child can learn to recognise and discriminate sounds that he hears, or is made able to hear, is quite a different matter. Tests of older children, who have already had remedial training, make clear the fact that variations in capacity to hear speech are found amongst those whose auditory acuity shows no difference (see our book *Teaching Deaf Children to Talk* (1964) and *The Education of Hearing-Handicapped Children* (1967) by Dr. J. T. Watson). We have met cases in which very deaf children, given much training from a very early age, have in time developed an important degree of capacity partially to recognise speech by hearing. For instance Brenda, who had home training from the age of two years, was profoundly deaf—average hearing level 105 decibels. She was having an individual auditory training lesson by her teacher, using a speech training hearing aid. Turning over a page her interest was attracted by a picture in which a child was shown to be wearing yellow shoes. Brenda pointed to the shoes. While she was still looking at the picture her teacher said, "She has yellow shoes". This Brenda instantly repeated, saying exactly the same words in the same manner with correct articulation. Knowing Brenda, it is extremely improbable that, on the basis of hearing alone, she would have recognised and discriminated the teacher's utterance if she had not had, at the same time, another set of cues to supplement those reaching her mind through her imperfect hearing. In this case, the cues came from the picture and her interest in it. Probably, also, as a result of all her previous training her mind was unconsciously drawing on memories of simultaneously hearing and lipreading her teacher making similar comments. There is a fundamental fact about our method that has enabled very severely deaf children, like Brenda, to make such valuable use of hearing. In many cases, certainly in Brenda's, sound was meaningless when training was first begun. The method is based on giving the children much experience of simultaneously hearing and lipreading spoken language in meaningful situations. In the next chapter we describe in detail methods of giving very young children at different ages experience that stimulates their minds to combine auditory and visual cues to identify sentences and words in spoken language.

All authorities on the development of spoken language in unhandicapped children agree on the importance to them of hearing their own voices. Even when left alone and in a happy mood, young babies, at a certain stage, can often be heard using their own voices, obviously enjoying the sound of them. As normal speech develops, hearing oneself speak becomes the essential means of controlling intonation, articulation and the loudness or quietness with which one talks. Onset of severe or total deafness, even long after learning to talk, can cause difficulty in this direction. For instance, an adult who has previously heard normally but becomes severely deafened can have very great difficulty in adjusting the loudness with which he talks in relation to background noise. He has become largely or totally unable to hear his own voice or the noise. Consequently it may be

47

extremely difficult for other people to hear what he says in such a place as a busy restaurant. By contrast, in a quiet room he may speak with unnecessary loudness. Special training can help to remedy this. The social skill involved here is one normally acquired, quite unconsciously, during childhood. Without knowing it, a child with unimpaired hearing who has learned to talk in the normal way gradually becomes accustomed to making himself adequately heard in varying acoustic conditions and according to the standards of his social environment.

Amongst hearing impaired children capacity to hear their own voices and speech varies widely. Deafness diagnosed as perceptive always reduces it in a lesser or greater degree. In our own researches we have found evidence that among deaf children under five, as well as those of school age, there is a significant number who hear their own voices only when well amplified. For example, we have described in Chapter One how Freda became accustomed to short periods of use of a speech training aid with her mother at home. It was then that she acquired a habit of vocalising as soon as a hearing aid was put on. Conversely, John, at about the same stage, would suddenly cease to use his voice if the microphone of the speech trainer was withdrawn.

All the information on this point emphasises a need to ensure that deafness in infancy is detected and diagnosed at the earliest possible age. Deaf children's use of their natural voices can only be maintained and developed by much effective experience of hearing their own vocalisations and beginnings of speech well amplified. Under this head many hard of hearing children have the same sort of need. With others, where it proves possible, once they have begun to talk there is a special need to amplify the weaker high-pitched components in speech.

Some children hear their own voices fairly well even without amplification but through its help and only through its help hear themselves articulate distinctly consonants like /s/ and /t/. Partial deafness of this kind is often reflected in a young child's articulation. He will have reached the stage of frequently putting words together. Perhaps he is talking in sentences. But it becomes noticeable that he is not getting beyond saying BU' for BUS, 'POON for SPOON, HOR' for HORSE, 'OAP for SOAP, etc. When the possibility of a young child's having a speech problem seems to be indicated by this sort of articulation and no test of hearing has previously been made parents should ask for one. But it should be remembered that /s/ has been found by eminent authorities on unhandicapped children's speech to be one of the five or six consonants that are most difficult to learn. It has even been reported that it may not be regularly and correcly used in a child's vocabulary until the ages of seven or eight. Nevertheless, because it is most often used by children with unimpaired hearing before they are five years old, it is advisable to have a hearing test if it is never used at all.

We believe that Dr. Mary Sheridan made a very important point when she stated in 1945 that she had found articulatory defects in young children are usually due to auditory confusions and not to muscular incoordination. She had studied the speech of 650 children under five years of age. We have referred previously to the category of children under five who are overtaken by hearing defects after having had normal auditory experience for two or three years. Not only may their deafness escape detection but also they have special needs of training. A great part of the risk for children who have heard normally during, say, the first three years of their lives is that most of them have learnt to talk and have become normally responsive to sound during those first years. Their behaviour has been normal and if partial deafness overtakes them the extent of the deprivation from which they have now begun to suffer is not nearly as obvious as when a similar degree of handicap has been present from birth. On medical grounds, as research in the 1960's has shown, investigation at consultant level is urgent if permanent damage in a certain number of cases is to be prevented. For under-fives who suffer a partial hearing impairment for any appreciable period of time guidance to parents about home training and management is of great importance to prevent delays in speech development and general mental growth.

Very special consideration as regards methods of early training has to be given to children diagnosed as having a hearing problem and also some other form of handicap. Sometimes they are mentioned as having "additional" or even "multiple" handicaps. The range of disability is very, very wide and so is the children's capacity to benefit from training. Our records include, for instance, the case of Joan, a child with very severe perceptive deafness and with a degree of cerebral palsy that, from infancy into adult life, has made one hand only usable as a holder. The leg on the same side is affected. She walks with a limp and has never been able to take part in active sport. Early home training was so successful that, with her mother's continued daily help, attendance at a normal school was justified after a period of individual education by a qualified teacher of the deaf. Full-time employment in a very responsible clerical post in industry was achieved. Both the early history and the follow-up into adult life, in this case, seem to indicate clearly that mental abilities were unimpaired. Joan had the capacity to benefit from all the excellent opportunities that were given to her and developed a secure, happy and well-adjusted personality.

Of course, not all hearing-impaired children with additional handicaps make good progress even when their condition is detected at an early age and guidance about training them is given to their parents. Problems for the parents themselves are inevitable and these we discuss in a later chapter. Among the children, a key factor seems to be the extent to which their innate mental abilities are affected. Before their abilities can be appreciated a period of remedial training, often for a considerable length of time, is usually essential. As Professor I. G. Taylor of Manchester University has high-lighted, the nervous systems of some children medically diagnosed as "brain-damaged" are late to mature.

As we have reported elsewhere a proportion of "multiply-handicapped" children included in our 1964 survey—about one-third—who were not talking when first seen had begun to talk after home training, before the age of five years. In this book when we say that a child is talking we mean that he has begun to use at least a small number of words spontaneously. This is not just on one or two occasions but consistently as a habit. The child, when he speaks in this way, can be recognised as using particular words to express particular meanings. If a child is only at the stage of imitating a parent or teacher on the spot we would not describe him as having got as far as talking.

Mandy, as an infant, presented a problem, fortunately, in our experience, not very frequently met. When first seen in a children's department of a hospital she was sixteen months old. She was found to be suffering from a bilateral atresia, that is there was no open passage to either ear. This was considered to be the result of her mother having taken the drug distaval during the pregnancy. The fact that there was a deformed thumb was an additional indication that this was one of those cases widely described as thalidomide. Initially she heard loud sound at 70 decibel level. That the inner ears were present was confirmed by X-ray examination. Her mother learnt to co-operate well in giving home training. By the age of two years Mandy was watching and listening when spoken to and had begun to make some attempts to imitate speech. By the age of four years seven months, when seen by a psychologist, Mandy "carried on long conversations with her mother". Her command and use of language was that of average children with unimpaired hearing one to two years younger than herself. In a performance test of intelligence her practical ability was found to be well above average (quotient 120). A recent operation on the left ear was found to have lessened the severity of her deafness (hearing level now 60 decibels).

In Mandy's case the absence of external openings to her ears proved to be the only specialised problem as regards her training. During her earlier years, when it was considered undesirable to undertake surgery, a body-worn hearing aid, of bone conduction type, was obtained for her. The head-band was cut down to the small size needed for a little child. With the portable speech training aid, lent to the parents for use in daily home training, the ordinary external receivers proved efficient.

John was another infant without external openings to his ears and with this handicap diagnosed as due to his mother's having taken thalidomide during the pregnancy. In his case, also, home training with amplification proved effective.

Walter's handicap was more complex. Like Mandy and John, there were no external openings to his ears but tests showed that he could hear very loud sound (low tones 80 decibels, high tones 60 decibels). The cause of his deafness was given a different diagnosis—the Treacher Collins Syndrome with its typical malformation of the lower jaw. An eminent authority, Professor R. I. Illingworth, has stated that none of the children with this syndrome, seen by him, were mentally normal. In Walter's case damage to the central nervous system was questioned. His rate of learning was slow and had to be taken into account in home training. By the age of three years ten months Walter had begun to talk spontaneously with a very limited vocabulary of words and word phrases. Before he went to school he had become able to talk in sentences. Of course, at both stages his understanding of what was said to him was ahead of what he could say himself.

Rachael when first seen at the age of seventeen months in a county audiology clinic showed no signs of beginning to talk. She was only vocalising to a limited extent. Speech addressed to her failed to arouse her attention. Rachael was referred to the Manchester University pre-school clinic. Medically she was diagnosed as having a heart lesion. Movement on the right side of her face was handicapped by a facial palsy and there was no external opening to the right ear. Home training was begun but medical opinion was that the facial palsy would prevent her from becoming able to talk. Rachael's parents were highly responsive to guidance. Their home training was so effective that she was later admitted to an ordinary primary school as a talking child. She was late in walking, indeed took her first steps without support at a parents' meeting in the University Clinic when she was two years one month old. It was found that hearing on the left side was, in fact, unimpaired. When she was two years ten months old she was talking in sentences of four words in length. It had been quite clear that in her case it had been essential to use home training methods to draw attention to speech.

Children popularly described as spastic have, in the past decade, received much public notice. There has been a great increase in the amount of attention given to their educational needs. In our own experience hearing impairment in association with deficiencies of the central nervous system present a range of very varying types of difficulty as regards early training and later education. Professor I. G. Taylor in his book *Neurological Mechanisms of Hearing and Speech in Children* (1964) reported instances of cerebral-palsied children who when tested before the age of one year were found unable to respond normally to sound but about two years later proved to be hearing very quiet sound. In such cases, as Professor Taylor and we ourselves have found, the children have to be freed from visual stimulation before they can respond to sound at minimal loudness. It should be mentioned, however, that in such cases this did not necessarily mean that the children had become able to discriminate normally between sounds and to understand speech. For instance, in one case

Professor Taylor reported that the child at the age of four "can only follow speech when there is situational guidance and then only if he can see the speaker's face".

Provision for training and education of cerebral-palsied children and studies of their potentialities and needs have chiefly been concentrated on those of school age. Earlier detection and diagnosis have presented a new challenge This at once involves the question as to how far parents can be guided to give such children home training. As has been stated by Mr. Sherwood A. Messner, Director of the Services Section, Medical and Scientific Department, United Cerebral Palsy Associations, City of New York, parents "need help in day-to-day management, in acceptance, in realistic goal-setting, and possibly in planning for eventual institutional placement". Where there is a defect of hearing there is also an imperative need to develop a cerebral palsied child's capacity for communication. This goal is additional to those listed for children obviously and profoundly brain-damaged, stated by Mr. Messner as "developing awareness of self and surroundings; increasing the level of motor activity; and developing self-help skills, especially in feeding, dressing and toileting". As experience with many deaf children in different categories has shown, personal communication is an extremely important factor in promoting development of perception—awareness of environment. It is similarly favourable to development of motor skills and activities. Conversely, particularly for young or immature children, it is direct practical experiences and activities which have meaning for them that provide the best means for developing communication.

Among the comparatively small number of hearing-impaired cerebral palsied children whom we have been able to study in detail and try to help some were regularly attending Rodney House, the Cerebral Palsy Nursery Clinic of the Manchester and District Spastic Society, under the care of Dr. Margaret Griffiths, Medical Officer in Charge. Day care centres in the U.S.A. provide similar services. When it is necessary for children to be in such centres for most of their days it is not easy for parents to find enough time, in their homes, for auditory training and development of understanding and use of spoken language. In any case, the task for parents is, of course, more difficult than the training of children whose hearing impairment is not associated with another handicap. There is always a problem that if for this or any other reason a child's progress in response to home training is slow his parents may become discouraged.

When Rose was eight months old she was referred to the Manchester University pre-school clinic because she was not responding to sound. By the time that she was twelve months old she was found to respond to both low and high pitched sound when rather loud—hearing level 60 decibels. Her mother had been guided to sing and talk close to Rose's ear. A hearing aid was prescribed but at that time ear-moulds were not immediately available, so that it was some months before it was regularly in use. When Rose had reached the age of fourteen months Professor I. G. Taylor had detected indications of cerebral palsy. This was diagnosed and found to be of the type known as athetoid. In pre-school home training this defect of the central nervous system—athetosis—involves special problems. The most obvious feature in behaviour, perhaps, is that of involuntary movements. These tend to increase when a child is under any stress. There is also unsteadiness and incoordination. In Rose's case sitting without support did not become possible until she was eighteen months old. Inability to sit up voluntarily limits a child's ordinary experience. It also limits possibilities of co-operative play even when body support is provided. Athetosis delays development of eye and hand co-ordination. For Rose this was further complicated by a convergent squint. Also, when an object is grasped it can be difficult to release it. At eighteen months it was still difficult for Rose to pick up a toy from a table. By the age of three and a half she was able to play with a toy tea-set, using real sugar and milk without spilling. Physio-therapy at the Rodney House Nursery Clinic helped her. Both to develop understanding of speech and talking, special methods were required. By the age of three and a half Rose was making recognisable attempts to say "thank you", "hello", and a few other words.

Not in all cases is it possible for home training to help towards development of communication.

Betty was another child diagnosed as suffering from the athetoid type of cerebral palsy. Her development was characterised by great capacity for persistence. Once able to walk at the age of four years five months she spent a good deal of her time enjoying that skill. At the age of three and a half she got about by crawling, chiefly shuffling along on her bottom. Precise assessments of her hearing before school age were difficult. Medical opinion at first was that she was aphasic. After eighteen months of home training beginning at the age of ten months, Betty was admitted to the Rodney House Nursery Centre. When she was three years three months old home training was resumed at the request of Dr. Griffiths. Perhaps one of the most useful results of home training was to bring about a positive interest in sound. For instance, at the age of four years, in the University Clinic, Betty found a xylophone for herself and played it. About the same age she had begun to watch as well as listen to simple speech in practical situations. When she was holding a doll and was given a brush she would look at her mother's face and wait for her mother to speak. Then, when asked, she would brush the doll's hair. Betty had a convergent squint. This was operated on but, in the opinion of a medical consultant who saw her later at the age of five, she had difficulty in gazing upwards. Betty was not talking at all by the age of five but, thanks to her capacity for persistence and all the help that had been given to her, she had become able to do a good deal for herself and would play happily, for instance with dolls. The progress that she was able to make may seem small but it was evidently worthwhile.

A child for whom different methods of home training were needed was Neil. He was eleven months old when we first saw him in a county audiology clinic. He had been diagnosed as blind because of a congenital cataract and also as a mongol seriously retarded in development. He was not responding normally to sound. During a subsequent period of less than two years we were able to see him from time to time. His mother was guided to use his sense of touch to help him to identify sources of selected sounds. For instance, a toy car was used to make a loud whirring noise with its wheels. He was helped to hold the car and feel its vibration while the wheels revolved. He was told "This is a car", and indeed "car" was one of the first words to appear in his expressive vocabulary. During the period in which his mother brought him to the University Clinic for guidance and assessment sessions there was evidence of greatly increased response to sound and of the growth of capacity to understand speech and to talk.

In this chapter we have tried to make clear the different needs of different children. In the next chapter our purpose is to explain and discuss in detail the different methods that have proved successful for the home training of the children.

4

Some methods in detail

To plan in detail methods of home training for a particular child the first step, for all concerned, is to make an objective assessment of what he can do—*now*. Needless to say, his chronological age is a main factor but whatever his age some simple questions are useful. To answer them, all of us who are concerned, as parents or otherwise, need to observe a child's behaviour in as detached and non-emotional a state of mind as possible.

(1) Physical development—Does he watch and follow with his eyes things that are being moved around him or in front of him? Does he reach for things that attract him, grasp them and let go of them? How much can he get about and how does he manage it?

(2) Mental growth—If he can handle things what does the child do with them? Does he throw things down, bang them or push them about? Does he put things together to make something, however simple, for instance building a tower with bricks. Has he some skills like throwing a ball where he wants it to go? Can he carry things? Will he look at pictures seeming to perceive their meaning or does he just flick over the pages of a picture book?

(3) Social behaviour—Is the child friendly? Does he seem a happy child most of the time? Does he sleep well? In keeping with his age does he co-operate with his parents? If he is old enough does he play with other children? Will he share toys? How does he communicate, for instance what does he

do when he wants something? Is he self-helpful—feeding, dressing, etc.?

(4) Hearing—Does he look up or look round when called to or in response to a sudden noise? How far, if at all, does he show clearly that he understands things which people say to him? If so, just what sort of things? Does he like to make noises himself—by shaking a rattle or by playing a xylophone? How much does he use his own voice and in what ways? Does he attempt any words and if so could a stranger recognise what he is saying?

All the methods of home training that we have proved successful, whatever the ages and conditions of the children, have involved three main principles. First, to help a child make use of all his sensory and motor abilities—watching, listening, doing. Because his hearing is imperfect we want him to have all possible cues as to what is going on. Second, to choose and use in right ways practical situations that encourage two-way talk. Third, as we have explained in Chapter Three, many hearing impaired children need skilled help and amplification which enables them to hear their own voices and, at least to some extent, their own speech as it develops. This is the principle, therefore, of stimulating use of the voice to ear link.

How in detail have we applied these three principles with infants before they were able to walk, manipulate objects purposefully or even sit unsupported? The very first step has often been to select and use things that will interest a baby when he sees them and cause him to take notice. When a child is handicapped by deafness there is less than normal stimulation to notice what is happening around him because of his inability to hear adequately the sounds made by people and things as they move about. The best way of all before the baby can sit without support is for a parent, granny or someone else to hold him looking forward while the other parent makes large lively movements with a brightly coloured and attractive toy, talking about them at the same time. The toy may be a teddy bear, a large red ball, a squeaking toy or a rattle that is in the form of an animal or a bird such as a rabbit or a duck. If no one is available to help, baby can be comfortably propped in his pram or cot or in an armchair or on a settee. There are two main objectives. One is to help baby to associate what he can see with what, as far as possible, he can be helped to hear. The other is to make use of a tendency that can develop naturally in babies at certain stages of growth. This is for an infant to watch the face of a person who is near him. Out of this, with the right handling, a hearing-impaired baby can be led to begin to gain cues from facial expression. This is a step on the way to beginning to lipread. In detail, let us think what it is best to do with a young baby, say seven to twelve months old. Mummy has been shown, perhaps in a clinic, how to move a teddy bear in such a way as to lead the baby to follow its antics. Daddy, or someone else, is holding baby on his knee facing towards her. When, because of what mummy is doing with the teddy, baby has become alerted and attentive, daddy speaks into his ear saying "Oh, look at teddy. What a lovely teddy he is!" Next mummy moves teddy to a position close to her face, ensuring that baby's gaze follows it. Daddy does not speak. Instead, mummy, talking clearly, not too quickly and very cheerfully repeats what daddy has said. (We describe later use of a hearing aid and microphone techniques.) If baby is able to hold the teddy bear mummy may follow up what she has already done by saying "Teddy is coming to you" before putting the toy within his reach. Experience of holding and feeling teddy will help in making the first beginnings of baby's approach to a concept or idea of it. The kind of method that we have outlined ensures that a baby is given visual, auditory and tactile cues as to what is happening, suitable to his stage of mental growth.

· We remember that such first steps in home training as we have described need to be taken every day and preferably several times a day. At this stage they should be of not more than ten minutes each. Mummy needs to employ all the ingenuity that she can in varying the ways in which she plays with particular toys. She needs also to vary the toys themselves, gradually collecting for the training periods a little store of toys which she finds she can make interesting to her baby.

There are a number of situations inevitable to the daily routines of care for a baby that can be almost or just as useful for home training as those just described. Mummy, when dressing baby, can make opportunities to say into his ear things like "These are your socks, nice warm socks." "Brush baby's hair." Whenever possible mummy will contrive to use with baby's socks, brush,

59

shoes, spoon, etc., this same method of winning his attention. She leads him to look at the objects and then again, as she holds one of them close to her face, talks about it, As always her facial expression needs to be lively.

We have found that even to a young baby it is always best to speak in sentences or phrases. There are several reasons. Normally, babies enjoy being talked to before they are able to understand what is said. The duration of the sentence that a person utters to them helps to draw attention to the sound of the voice and to the speaker. When a baby is known to be deaf or hard of hearing there is always a risk that people, including his parents, may talk to him in a way that is unnatural, perhaps in single words. When they talk to him in simple sentences they are much more likely to speak with natural rhythm and intonation with accompanying changes of facial expression, all of which help to attract the baby's attention and to make him feel that people and their faces matter. The importance, to a deaf baby, of learning to look at faces cannot in our opinion be over-emphasised. In this way it will be natural for him to grow ready to lipread, an ability that all hearing-impaired children need to acquire and use, at least in some circumstances.

It is normal for most mothers to sing to their babies while rhythmically rocking or jogging them in time with their singing. We have found that hearing-impaired babies can also enjoy this. For a baby under the age of twelve months who, when first tested, appears to be severely or profoundly deaf, or even totally deaf, auditory training has often been begun by talking and sometimes singing into his ear. Sometimes a baby who had seemed to be totally deaf has begun, after this training, to respond to sound. Some babies have been observed, later on, to jog themselves up and down when their mothers sing. A similar association between passive movement and sound can be given by holding the baby's hands in one's own and moving his arms gently up and down as one speaks or sings into his ear, on the better side if there is known to be a difference in acuity between the ears. Some children show by smiling that they enjoy this form of play. Of course these methods are equally useful with hard of hearing babies.

To build up the habit of combining listening with watching hearing aids are necessary. For lipreading it is best for one's eyes

SOME METHODS IN DETAIL

to be at least three feet from the face of a speaker. Also, for a little child, the speaker's face needs to be on the same level as his own. It is not only movements of lips and mouth that give visible cues as to what a person is saying. Expression and movements of the face as a whole make available a combination of cues. What all this comes to is that for a baby with any considerable degree of deafness the sound of singing or speech needs to be amplified by a hearing aid to make it adequately audible to him at lip-reading distance.

As regards hearing aids, in this chapter we are concerned solely with methods of using them. The main principles apply with little modification to all children under five. Settings of the volume control and of the tone control, if fitted, will have been recommended by an expert, probably a qualified audiologist in a clinic. As home training proceeds an initial setting may be revised. When a body-worn aid is to be used in home training the cord or flex from the main unit of the aid to the child's earpiece needs to be about thirty-six inches or one metre in length. This long cord makes it possible for a parent to use the body-worn hearing aid as a hand microphone that can be held by an adult below his or her chin, speaking at not more than four inches from it but not hiding any part of the face. The long flex can quickly be exchanged for a shorter one at other than special training periods if the child is to wear the aid throughout the day.

To gain the best possible results from a hearing aid for their own child parents need to remember three things—in addition to the recommended volume setting or settings:

(a) always to speak with a clear voice, rather more loudly than in ordinary quiet conversation;
(b) to speak distinctly and yet with natural rhythm in sentences or phrases;
(c) to speak more slowly than is usual in modern quick conversation.

Some simple professional training in a clinic can be very helpful towards achieving the three aims that we have just listed. This can include, very usefully indeed, practice with a sound-level meter of the portable kind often used in industry as well as by audiologists.

61

Besides hearing other people's voices babies need to hear their own. For a deaf child this is crucial. In parent guidance sessions we have seen very young deaf children who were obviously enjoying the sound of their own voices, when amplified by a hearing aid, become silent and stay silent when the aid was switched off. Without amplification many of the young children who are deaf or hard of hearing do not hear enough of their own voices to stimulate and encourage them to use them. So in special home training times provision needs to be made for this. With a baby whose vocalisations are necessarily spontaneous and may occur at any moment a parent has to be ready quickly to transfer a microphone from her own mouth to the child's. Again, the distance of the microphone from the child's mouth should usually be not greater than about four inches.

There is another kind of hearing aid which, since it first became available, we have always found most valuable in home training. It is the kind known as a speech training aid or auditory training unit. The best models are fitted with two microphones. One of these can be hung round the adult's neck, thus making it easy for the parent either to have both hands free for manipulation of toys or, probably most of the time, to be holding it near her mouth. The other microphone, as soon as the child is old enough, can be hung round his neck. To hang a microphone round the neck is much more effective in home training than to use it standing on a table. The first reason for this is to ensure to the child continuous experience of the voice to ear link. The second is the desirability of keeping table space free for toys.

An even more important advantage of this type of aid is, as we show in Chapter Six, that good models have a much better performance than is possible with body worn hearing aids. There is greater high fidelity. Part of the means for this is that a child hears through external, on-ear telephone receivers which, when of good quality, offer excellent reproduction of sound to both ears. Loudness levels at each ear can be precisely and separately regulated to suit a child's needs. The receivers are normally worn on a head-band adjustable in size.

In practice, we have not infrequently found that a training aid of this kind is the best means of giving a very young child his first experience of amplification. It makes possible a very

SOME METHODS IN DETAIL

gradual introduction to use of a hearing aid. The child is watching, in front of him, what his mother is doing with an attractive noise-making toy. She may be playing a xylophone in a lively way, singing in time with the music that she makes with it. If the child needs much amplification she uses one hand to hold her microphone close to the noise-making toy—in this case the xylophone. Her helper, the training aid having been switched on, holds one of the receivers near the child's ears—the better ear if a difference between them has been found. With the child's attention still focused on the toy, the receiver is slowly moved nearer and nearer to his ear, finally to cover it. When this method has been used several times we have found that a young child, severely deaf, may come to press his ear against the receiver, without waiting for it to be placed there by the adult. There could not be clearer proof of a deaf child's awareness and enjoyment of becoming able to hear as well as to see what is happening. The method by-passes a risk of what is liable to occur with some, not all, young children, rejection of the unfamiliar sensation of something touching an ear. Most very young children, if fitted with a headset and not given the kind of preparation that we have outlined, immediately pull it off. It is better for them to learn to accept a headset voluntarily than for them to be emotionally upset by having it in any way forced upon them. When they have found that a thing placed on the ear gives them the pleasure of hearing sound from a recognisable source they are far more likely to accept the ear-mould and insert-receiver of a body-worn hearing aid that provides them with similar experience.

Here, perhaps, mention should be made of a technical problem that is liable to occur when a child needs a high level of amplification. This is the possibility of a whistling sound which comes from the receiver of a hearing aid when its volume control is set to give loud sound and the sound from the receiver is being picked up by the microphone and re-amplified. The resulting whistle, technically described as acoustic feed-back, needs to be prevented. It is not just a disagreeable and distracting noise. What is worse, it distorts the sound that the hearing aid is being employed to amplify. An ill-fitting ear-mould with a body-worn aid also leaks back sound to the microphone. For this there is only one radical cure which is to have a better fitting ear-mould made. It is essential, also, that an ear-mould should not be a cause of discomfort.

With a training aid two methods help to ensure prevention of acoustic feed-back. First, if the receiver is uncovered and gradually being held closer and closer to a very young child's ear, as we described further back in this chapter, to take care not to bring the microphone needlessly near to the receiver. Secondly, when the headset of a hearing aid is being worn by a child and a high level of amplification is to be used, not to switch on the sound until the receivers have been correctly fitted.

To avoid risk of frightening a child, by what may seem to him a sudden and unfamiliar stimulus, volume settings are carefully selected. With a very young child it is a great help for tests to have been made in an audiology clinic to find, as accurately as possible, just how loud sound needs to be made to be just audible. The most satisfactory precedure seems to be to start a child's experience of hearing through an aid with a volume setting that gives him sound of one's voice at a loudness level that is ten decibels greater than the level at which it is just detectable, that is, just audible. This level is often described as the "threshold of detectability". It helps a lot to use at the start a training aid with a meter on its control panel. With this a parent or teacher can monitor her way of speaking so as to talk with the clear and not too quiet voice that will cause the aid to give the best kind of reproduction of which it is capable. When the child has grown accustomed to the amount of amplification that we have just described a further increase of ten decibels may be tried, with caution. Careful watch is made for any indication, in the child's facial expression or general behaviour, that his physical or his mental capacity to tolerate very loud sound are being exceeded, in which case an immediate reduction of 10 decibels in volume setting is effected. Often a setting of 30 decibels above voice detectability threshold proves best in the end. With young children, this technique is the only means known to us of ascertaining their optimum volume settings.

We hope that we have made clear the advantages of beginning the home training of very young children who are at all severely deaf by using speech training aids or auditory training units. The practice of having a supply of them in clinics for lending to parents has steadily grown.

Optimum volume settings for little children who need body-worn hearing aids are less easy for a parent to find at all accurately. It is not usual for body-worn aids to have volume controls that indicate levels of soundness according to a decibel scale. As has been already advised initial volume settings are best selected in a clinic by an audiologist who will take into account the individual child's thresholds of detectability as found during tests of hearing for speech and other sounds.

In all cases in which sound has to be made very loud indeed to reach a young child's threshold of detectability expert guidance is needed about adjustment of volume controls. Both in the University pre-school clinic and at the Royal Schools for the Deaf, at Manchester, we ourselves have had responsibility for young children whom we are obliged to describe as very severely deaf indeed. Some of them were greatly helped in learning to talk by high levels of the right kind of amplification—in home training and also at school—but it had to be very knowledgeably and skilfully used.

The amount of noise present in a room or out of doors needs to be taken into account. We would say that, to all very young children and older ones too, it is advisable to give the opportunity, in the first stage of training, to get used to a hearing aid in really quiet conditions. If a child is inexperienced, a sudden loud noise coming through a hearing aid may cause fright and discomfort. As an audiologist will explain, defective hearing does not carry exemption from overloading of the ears. Much overloading may affect the efficiency of hearing for short or for longer periods of time.

Use of hearing aids in noisy conditions, such as may obtain in some family situations at home, in a play group or in school, calls for careful consideration and management. The problem is similar to that of listening, on a televised or radio programme, to speech transmitted from a noisy street with traffic rushing past. For a child using a hearing aid the difficulty of following speech which is already complicated by much noise is further increased by the deficiencies of his own hearing. The best method of coping, if it is at all practicable, is for anyone who is speaking to him to talk close to the microphone. This method can be used to make the speech as picked up by the microphone more distinct and louder than the noise. It is a technique commonly

65

adopted by commentators on sports programmes. Often when hearing aids have to be used in noisy or reverberant conditions volume controls cannot wisely be set to give as much amplification as is best for the child in a very quiet room.[1]

When using a hearing aid, it is helpful to a deaf child to experience many kinds of movement in which he can see it, hear the sound that accompanies it and feel its vibrations. Once children find that with simple sound-making toys, such as rattles, xylophones and drums, they can make sound that they can hear through aids, they greatly enjoy doing so. The microphone of the hearing aid needs to be held close to the sound-making toy. When an auditory training unit is used its volume controls should be set to give a moderate gain above a child's threshold of detectability and the loudness of the sound input should be monitored with the meter on the control panel.

A very effective way of beginning to evoke spontaneous use of voice from a young child has proved to be for an adult, holding a toy car, to move it across the table saying rather loudly as she does so "Br-r-r-r-r——". Many children, in response, have taken the car and tried to imitate the noise as well as the movement. Similarly, flying up in the air an attractive-looking aeroplane, the adult may say "Oo——" making her voice rise in pitch as the aeroplane goes up and lower in pitch as the plane comes down.

In all auditory training of young children understanding and experience are needed to use the "psychological moment" when a child is ready to respond to a new variation in his experience. This means, as a rule, that it must not be offered to him when he is already preoccupied in some other way. It is so important to his social development that he should learn to look to his mother or a teacher as someone who brings him new and enjoyable experience, not as someone who is constantly interfering with what he is already doing.

This is particularly true as hearing-impaired babies become toddlers. If a mother–child relationship that involves, on a child's part, listening and looking for speech, has been established before he begins to walk unsupported and move about a room, so much the better. If he has already learnt to listen and look he is the more ready and willing to sit down for short periods

[1] The subject of noise is further discussed in Chapter Six.

of home training that involve co-operative play at a table. This makes use of a training aid possible throughout the play. The table needs to be a low one. Mother and child sit opposite each other with mother's face at or about the same level as the child's. This makes it possible to combine lipreading with hearing. By about the age of fifteen months a child can learn to "Push the ball (or motor car, etc.) to mummy", "Now push the ball to daddy (or John or Susan)".

Control of the toys must be kept by the parent to avoid breakdown of the co-operative situation through the child's becoming involved in free play. To hold the child's spontaneous interest and attention the adult has to keep the situation moving by contriving a continuous series of happenings and things for the child to do, making sure that all of them are linked with talking. In an early stage of home training a child's natural pleasure in making banging noises can be utilised. One suggestion is for mother to begin by holding up the base of a hammer and peg toy, close to her face. Speaking close to her microphone, she may say "Look at all these holes", poking a finger into them. Then "You have it" and she gives the base to the child. Quickly she produces a peg, holds it close to her face and says "Here's a peg. You have a peg." While the child is taking the peg she picks up the base. Then holding it and pointing to a hole she says "Put the peg in the hole" and places the base on the table in front of the child. At once the mother produces the hammer. Going through the same procedure as before she says to the child "You hammer the peg". Without any unnecessary delay she produces some more pegs, one after the other, and each time follows the same procedure. An important advantage here is that the child is given repetitions of the same sentences in conditions in which the associated acts of doing make them meaningful. This principle is very important to his learning to understand spoken language as a basis for beginning to use it himself.

A similar procedure can be followed to contrive co-operative play-and-talk situations with a posting box, building a tower with bricks, linking together, wagon by wagon, a train set, inserting little men in a boat. These are a few suggestions to help parents to collect a small range of toys suitable for co-operative play-and-talk with children at an early stage in development of manual dexterity. The bigger the variety of toys that can be assembled the better. Different toys used on different days are a means to stimulate lively interest in a child. It is well worth while to take any and all opportunities of enabling him to hear a noise natural to movement of a toy. During building of a tower, for instance, bricks can be heard to "click" on to each other, if the microphone is held close to them.

We have found that co-operative play-and-talk periods with a training unit, by initiating a very young child's response to sound in his environment, can facilitate acceptance of a hearing aid as something to be worn from the time of dressing in the morning until that of undressing at night. All day use of an aid makes it possible for a parent to attract a child, indoors or out-of-doors, to look at something that is making a noise which is known by now to be likely to be audible to him through his hearing aid. Within the home a child's attention may be usefully attracted to sound made by mother in the kitchen, for instance when breaking and beating an egg, chopping something, running water when she turns on a tap, switching on the washing machine. There are other indoor sounds that can be used—the noise of a typewriter or sewing machine, daddy hammering or sawing, an electric razor, a dog barking or a cat mewing. Out-of-door sounds in the same sort of category can include those of an approaching lorry, motor-cycle or train, a lawn-mower, a hedge-cutter, the sirens, with flashing lights, of a police car, a fire-engine or ambulance. In general the volume controls of children's hearing aids should be set to give appreciably less amplification in noisy town conditions than in a quiet home. Of course, in the country, farm animals give good opportunities. Proof of the value of this sort of thing was offered by an older child, who, severely deaf, when taken to a farmyard wearing her hearing aid, was standing close to and watching a cow. Suddenly the cow lowed and the child called out "I saw the cow moo". There was another time when a little boy, very severely deaf, was surprised to hear as well as see a cock crowing.

The mother of a two-year-old can contrive many brief opportunities, some perhaps only a minute or so in duration, for promoting his speech comprehension. In all the routines of dressing and undressing, meals and going out to shop, as well as in very active play when the child is moving about the room or a garden, his mother trains him to look at her face when she speaks to him at varying distances. He will be wearing his hearing aid and his mother will get to know at what distance he can hear the sound of her voice with it. Incidentally to all daily happenings —when for instance they are going to the shops—the mother tells the child what is going to happen. She asks him to do things and puts into words for him what he, and other people, animals and things have done.

The advantages for all children, of reaching a stage of what we call "speech readiness" by the age of two years, are very great. When a child whose hearing is defective has begun to vocalise purposefully because he desires to communicate definite wants to other people, he is ready to be encouraged to try to repeat very simple phrases, appropriate to the circumstances. For example, when a two-year-old vocalises and gestures that he wants a toy car, his mother, holding it near her face says "The car, please". At the first occasion on which this happens the child may make no obvious attempt to repeat what she has said, but if she and other people contrive that similar situations occur frequently, a time will come when he begins, however imperfectly, to repeat her words. The mother always takes care to speak to the child in phrases and sentences but she will of course, accept from him at this early stage single words like "car", however imperfectly articulated. It is most important for her to show to him clearly how pleased she is with his attempts to talk.

In the next stage of home training the aim is to help the child to a more advanced level of communication and thinking related to a wider range of activities and interests. This is especially done during the training periods at the table. In the first stage the parent limited the number of toys in use at any time to two or three. Something was being done with each of them. After each toy had served its purpose it was put away out of sight. This avoided the risk that the child might resort to free play with it and that the co-operation of child with parent in play-and-talk might break down.

But as soon as a habit of co-operation with a child has been built up and when he has come to realise that play with his mother is enjoyable she can begin to leave on the table toys that she and the child have already used together. Gradually she accustoms him to concentrating his attention selectively. Now the mother still limits the number of toys but carefully plans to use the same ones in a growing number of ways and in different situations. For instance a little baby doll can be bathed, put to bed, have its hair brushed, given a bottle, put on a chair, put in a pram. Mother presents each toy by the same methods as in the beginning stages of home training, using the same microphone techniques. Having assembled in this way a group of toys her aim now is for the child to learn to understand and carry out what she asks when that entails his picking up and doing something with one or two toys and leaving others, for the moment, untouched. With repetition and careful management the time will come when the child will have learnt to recognise what is wanted without the mother's needing to hold the toys, that have already been used, near her face. By the time this stage is reached children have usually formed a habit of listening and looking up to lipread. Also, by now, they are usually attempting to copy some of the words of which they know the meaning.

At this point it is very much worth while to encourage the child's attempts to talk by further changing the method. This time mother holds up the baby, close to her face, saying "Where shall we put the baby?" The child, of course, has the choice of the bath, the bed, the chair, the pram, etc. His first attempts at replying may be by pointing to one of the items. Mother then helps and encourages him to try to name the item. It is useful for mother to bring out a family of dolls, one by one—father, mother, boy, girl. As previously with the baby, she says "Where shall we put Mummy?" (daddy, the boy, the girl).

We have stressed before that in home training we have found it best for adults to speak to children in simple sentences and phrases, not in single words. It is as a result of this that a stage is reached at which the children begin to try to speak more than one word at a time. A key point about the method that we have just described has proved to be that after a child, for instance, has replied "Chair" in response to mother's question "Where shall we put the boy?", mother immediately says, "Yes, on the chair". Then, when the child has put the boy on the chair the mother says "Good. You put the boy on the chair." This can be done without causing any sense of frustration in the child's mind. We have found that the kind of preliminary training that we have described makes it natural for a child to look up to his parent when he has done something, perhaps hoping for approval communicated to him by his parent's facial expression.

For all children, learning to understand spoken language precedes ability to use it in talking. The learning is mostly very gradual and is usually a result of frequent repetitions of the same phrases and sentences addressed to them on different occasions. It may be quite a while before a baby will wave a hand when mother says "Wave bye-bye". Later still, and after further repeated experience, he not only waves his hand but himself says "Bye-bye".

Some suggestions may be helpful as regards the kinds of small toys for use in play-and-talk periods at the table with the training unit. They need, of course, to be easy to move about and individual items must not take too much space. To make more room available on the play-table the training unit may need to be placed on another table or chair drawn up beside it. All the toys listed below have, in fact, been included in the home training of English children, under our guidance. All of them have been obtainable at small cost in English toy shops, but mostly as a result of looking for them in different shops on different occasions, or buying one if one happens to see it and if one thinks that it may come in useful in the future. "Never lose an opportunity" is a good motto!

Some items can obviously be introduced into more than one setting, e.g. trees into a garden or a farm or the zoo; similarly a dog can be part of the set-up of both indoor and out-of-door scenes; a car is all right in an airport or a farm set, as well as for the street scene or a garage. The number of items that it is suitable to include at any one time depends on the extent and growth of the child's vocabulary in relation to the scene and subject in use. One begins with only a few items and adds more as the child's understanding and interest increase.

Our list includes:

Household scenes with furniture of the kind used in different rooms. At first we use the articles to represent in play the activities normal to the life of a very young child. A tea-set gives opportunities for pretending to "Pour out the tea", "Put in some sugar", "Pour in some milk", "Stir the tea", "Drink the tea", "Give mummy a drink", "Give the dolly a drink". Some small children much enjoy sets with which to bath the baby, dry it with a towel, brush its hair, give it a bottle and put it to bed or in the pram. Particular sets of items can lead in time to the child's coming to know the names of different rooms in a house —lounge, kitchen, bedroom, bathroom, etc. Rooms can be arranged, item by item, on a table.

A very effective and attractive way of adding realism, interest and unity to a scene, we have found, is to make a base for it. A large sheet of cardboard is coloured to represent paths and lawns for a garden; fields, paths, a pond and a river for a farm or a zoo; a road with pavements or side-walks for a street scene. Suggested toys for such scenes are:

A garden—a house (easily made), trees, strips to represent flower beds, a garden seat, lawn mower, roller, a spade, a rake, a dog, a cat, people, a swing, hedges.

A farm—farm animals, ducks and hens, fences and hedges, trees, a pail to feed animals or fill with water from the pond, a tractor, a cattle van, other farm vehicles, a farmer and his wife, a bridge for the river.

A zoo—various animals, some to use a pond represented on the base, trees, cages, fences, keepers and other people, a bridge.

A petrol (gas) station—a garage building, office kiosk, pumps, attendant and other people, cars and other vehicles including a tanker.

Other scenes that we would suggest for similar builds-up would include a railway station, an airport, a street scene and a seaside scene. Readers, no doubt, will think of other possibilities.

A very practical point about all the scenes that we have suggested is that they relate to real life. Actual visits to them increase the children's interest and give a normal kind of encouragement to use of the relevant vocabularies, both by them and by the parents.

Most children come to be interested in picture books. They can offer a very wide variety of situations and vocabulary. They need using skilfully when brought into home training. It is natural for a parent and a child to enjoy picture books together. We would suggest that they are brought in while children are using their wearable hearing aids. A little child may be sitting on his mother's knee or seated beside her on a settee, looking at a book with her, or in bed before he goes to sleep. The main point, of course, is the way a parent utilises each picture to make conversation between himself (or herself), and the child. The situation is one that affords an excellent opportunity of encouraging and leading the child to join in two-way conversation. At the very beginning it is likely that the parent does the talking. "That's a big dog!" says the parent, drawing the child's attention by pointing to that particular feature of the picture. "Look at the bird on that tree!" "Oh, and there's a bird flying away." "The little boy is on the swing." "There's his daddy pushing the swing." As always, our method is for the adult to speak in a phrase or sentence rather than single words. We have found that sooner or later this way of talking about pictures stimulates hearing-impaired children to try to do the same thing. A severely deaf child will often begin by making what seem like spontaneous exclamations in single words imperfectly articulated—(h)or(se) or (c)ar or boa(t). Whenever this sort of thing happens a parent immediately takes the chance of repeating in an encouraging manner, "Oh yes, that's a horse." or "Yes, it's a big car" or "That's a lovely boat". This technique has the great advantage of putting the child's thought and attempt to express it into natural and more acceptable language.

When, as we have suggested, the situation is one in which the child is using his own wearable hearing aid, in many cases it will help a child for the parent to use it as a hand microphone. With a little child, say on mother's knee, speaking into the better ear can often offer a very good alternative to artificial amplification. Joan, to whom we have referred in Chapter Three, has emphasised to us that she benefited greatly over a long period of her childhood from her mother's daily practice of spending some time talking directly into her ear. As we have already reported Joan suffers from lifelong deafness, severe and perceptive in type.

Our readers will have noted that our recommendations indicate that the phrases and sentences in which parents talk to their children, even in the earliest stages, are colloquial and by no means formal. There is no question of beginning only with the naming of people and things. When the adult's intention, at a particular moment, is to help a child to learn and later to use a name he may emphasise it, but it is, nevertheless, presented as part of a sentence that normally might be addressed to an un-handicapped child of the same age. The number of words in the sentence—its length—needs to be adjusted, of course, to the maturity of the child and to the stage that he has reached in learning to talk. To a two-year-old very deaf child at the beginning of his home training a parent might say at a meal, "Here's your milk" with emphasis on the word *milk* but without in any way separating it from the rest of the sentence. Similarly, to the same two-year-old one might say "I'll put some jam on your bread", stressing the word *jam*. To a four-year-old who has already made good progress through early home training a parent will say "Would you like some sauce with your fish?" with emphasis on the word *sauce*. There might be occasion to say to the child, "Be careful with that knife. It's very sharp", with emphasis on both the words *careful* and *sharp*.

Grammatically speaking, different parts of speech, not just nouns and names, are needed to match with the growth of a young child's experience and thinking. As Dr. Dorothea McCarthy of the University of Minnesota and others after her have found, unhandicapped children actually use at least as many verbs and other parts of speech as nouns from the age of three years on-wards. In home training a key point is that young children are particularly interested in something happening, something being done. As our illustrations have shown this interest is our motive and means for using verbs in talking to hearing-impaired children from the very beginning of home training. Necessarily, some of the words that we emphasise in our sentences are verbs. Playing with a teddy bear, to interest a young baby, one might say "Watch teddy jump" with emphasis on the word *jump* and proceed to make it do so. Or, playing with a brightly coloured ball on a table, one says "I'll push the ball to you", with emphasis on the word *push*. (This, incidentally, is preparing the baby for the time when he will become able to push the ball himself and one can say "Push the ball to me".) Similarly, to talk about many of the do-ings that are naturally suitable to home training and others that are inevitable to a young child's daily routines, adjectives, preposi-tions and adverbs are needed. Most pronouns and all conjunc-tions, perhaps, come a little later. Indeed, some of the samples that we have given in this chapter illustrate this principle.

We hope that our readers will find it helpful to have the following word for word reports of these principles when applied in actual home training by the mothers of two children. In both cases we have used transcriptions from tape recordings included in those made at intervals as part of our normal procedure for parent guidance. Here we are giving sentence by sentence, what the mothers said, just as they said it. We have not thought it necessary for our immediate purpose to attempt a phonetic transcription of the children's responses and spontaneous utterances.

Karen, the first child, was sub-totally deaf. Even with the auditory trainer that her mother was using speech could only be made audible to her to a very limited degree. Lipreading, of course, was essential. Her age at the time of recording was 3 years 2 months. By the time that she went to school—months later— she was a talking child, although her vocabulary was quite modest and articulation imperfect.

The recording shows clearly how well Karen's mother gained her co-operation. She was using for this particular bit of home training a constructional toy, new to the child. The mother involves Karen in assembling parts of the motor car and putting into it little figures of people. She stimulates and holds Karen's attention by always keeping things moving. This kind of control is essential at times set apart by a parent for giving auditory training and developing spoken language. It is evident that Karen is not at all frustrated but is enjoying having her mother play with her.

Mother: Here's a motor-car.
Karen says "motor-car" with good rhythm but without consonants.
Mother: Motor-car, yes.
(Thus she responds to Karen's imperfect utterance by repeating it back to her correctly.)
Mother: Put the wheels on. Put them on. (Note introduction of pronoun.)
Karen attempts to say "put on".
Mother: Put them on there and we press and we press.
Karen approximates "press".
Mother: Press. Karen, we'll push them on. Push them on. We push them on.
Karen approximates "push".
Mother: Here's the wheels for the motor-car. Here's the wheels for the motor-car.
Karen approximates "wheels motor-car".

75

Mother—repeating correctly the phrase attempted by the child: The wheels for the motor-car.

Mother: And we push it in. You push the wheel in now. You push the wheel in.

Karen approximates "in".

Mother: Push it in, Karen. Push it in. (Karen pushes the wheel in.) That's a clever girl. (Tones of voice show praise.) You say clever girl. (No attempt by Karen to say this.) Here's the windows. Here's the windows. We push them on. Push them on. Press.

(Karen helps her mother to press on the car windows.)

Mother: You do it now. You put the windows in. You put the windows on the motor-car.

Karen says "motor-car" imperfectly but, in the context, intelligibly.

Mother: Here's the windows, Karen. Here's the windows for the motor-car. Put them on. Put them on the motor-car.

Karen approximates "on the motor-car", uttering five syllables.

Mother: Put them in. You press it in now. *You* press it in (note mother's emphasis on the pronoun. Karen presses in the window). That's clever. (Tones of voice show praise.)

Karen, this time, approximates "clever".

Mother: (Giving back the correct speech patterns.) That's clever. Say press. Press. Press them in. (Karen makes no attempt to say press, so her mother changes the word.) Push, push, you say push.

Karen approximates "push".

Mother: That's right. Oh! here's daddy.

Karen imperfectly says "daddy".

Mother: That's clever. Put him in. Put him in. (Again changing a word.) Push him in. Push.

Karen co-operates.

Mother: Karen say sit down. Say sit down.

Karen approximates "Say sit down", clearly uttering three syllables.

Mother: (giving back the correct speech pattern). Sit down. Sit daddy there. (Karen does so.) Oh! is the motor-car going? Put mummy in the motor-car, then.

Karen attempts to repeat "put mum motor-car", with approximate articulation.

Mother: (giving Karen the correct speech pattern of the whole sentence). Put mummy in the motor-car.

Karen tries to put mummy in the car but daddy falls out.

Mother: Oh! daddy fell out. Daddy fell out. Sit mummy in. Sit mummy in.

Karen puts mummy in the car.

Mother: Sit down, mummy. (Purposely repeating the phrase that she had spoken about daddy.) Oh! daddy keeps falling out.

Karen, spontaneously utters three syllables, seeming to approximate "Oh! sit down".

Mother: Sit down.

Karen approximates "sit down", then apparently "Oh! sit down" with quite a natural rise and fall in the pitch of her voice.

Mother: Sit down. She's sat down now. Look, yes, she's sat down.

Karen approximates she's sat down.

Mother: (Presumably holding a figure of a girl close to her face.) Here's Karen.

Karen approximates "here's Karen".

Mother: Put Karen in the motor car.

Karen approximates "Karen motor car", then spontaneously and evidently pointing to the little girl's dress attempts to say "dress".

Mother: Yes, that's Karen's dress. That's right. (Mother holds a second little girl close to her face.) Here's Jacintha. Put Jacintha in the motor car.

Karen approximates Jacintha.

Mother: Jacintha. Say Jacintha.

Karen again approximates Jacintha.

Mother: Jacintha. Put Jacintha in the motor car. (Karen does so.) That's right. That's clever. That's a clever girl.

Karen approximates "clever girl".

Mother: They're all in the motor car. Daddy fell. Daddy fell out.

Mother: (producing a cardboard base coloured to represent a road with grass fields on each side). Is it going down the road now? All going down the road. (Picking up the car she holds it near her face.) Here's the motor car, the motor car, Karen.

Karen approximates motor car.

Mother: (imitating the noise of a car as she pushes it down the road) b-r-r-r, b-r-r-r.

Karen, holding out her hand, approximates "car" twice. (Her mother gives it to her and Karen pushes it down the road.)

Mother: The motor car going down the road. Is it your car? Say "my car".

Karen approximates "car" with an initial consonant.

Sally

Our next transcription shows how Sally's mother was giving her home training with a speech training aid when she was 3 years 6 months of age. As we have reported in the first chapter of this book Sally suffered from high-tone deafness and without amplification could just hear, very faintly and intermittently, some sound of a male voice at a level of 65 decibels. This is the maximum level of loudness reached by the stronger vowels in moderately loud conversation at a distance of three feet. Sally is profoundly deaf to some of the higher pitched sound that conveys many con-

77

sonants. As home training proceeded it was very evident that when using a speech trainer the extent to which she could hear the sound patterns of speech was increased to include valuable versions of consonants.

This next transcription illustrates well the beginnings of two-way conversation between parent and child. As will be seen Sally sometimes makes spontaneous suggestions about use of the toys, indeed even questions what her mother does with them. The mother–child relationship is very good and there is no frustration on the part of Sally in her session at the play-table using the speech training hearing aid. In the tape recording Sally's articulation often approximates closely to that of a normal child of her age.

Mother: What's this?
Sally: Fire
Mother: A fire-place.
Sally: A fire p(l)ace.
Mother: There's the fire-place. (Giving it to Sally.)
Sally: Fire. In the living-room?
Mother: In the living-room. Right.
Sally: In the living-room.
Mother: That's the living-room.
Sally: The living-room.
Mother: And here's the settee.
Sally: For Wendy?
Mother: What is it?
Sally approximates very imperfectly "settee".
Mother: Yes.
Sally: And this is for Mark.
Mother: Wendy, Malcolm and Mark.
Sally: In the living-room.
Mother: In the living-room on the settee.
Sally: And the fire.
Mother: The fire-place.
Sally: Lounge.
Mother: Oh, is that the lounge?
Sally: The lounge.
Mother: The lounge, yes. What's this?
Sally: Sally's chair.
Mother: Sally's chair. What colour is it?
Sally: A red chair.
Mother: Yes.
Sally: That's a red chair. (She drops it.)

Mother: Oo-, you dropped it.
Sally: That's a red chair. (Having picked it up.)
Mother: Sit Sally on the chair.
Sally: Sally?
Mother: Yes.
Sally: That Mark.
Mother: No, that's Mark. This is Sally.
Sally: Oo-oo-oo. (As she accidentally knocks over the toys.)
Mother: Everything's fallen over.
Sally: No, that one's Mark.
Mother: Oh, that one's Mark, is it?
Sally: That one's Mark. Mark, that Mark.
Mother: And who's that one?
Sally: Malcolm. Here's Mark.
Mother: Yes. We'll put that one in the chair here.
Sally: That one's ... Rest of her sentence masked by noise of toys falling. Oh!
Mother: Oh dear! oh dear! Who's this? Who's this?
Sally: Duncan.
Mother: Is that Duncan? No, this is too big for Duncan. That one's Sally.
Sally: Duncan, Duncan.
Mother: Here's Duncan. Here's Duncan.
Sally: That baby.
Mother: That's Duncan.
Sally: Here. (Placing the toy.)
Mother: In a high chair.
Sally: In a high chair.
Mother: Yes, in a high chair.
Sally: Sally's chair and Duncan's chair.
Mother: That's Duncan's chair. Is he going to have some tea? What's this? It's a blue mug.
Sally: Blue mug.
Mother: Put the milk in.
Sally: Milk. For Duncan. (She is heard to manipulate the toy.) Jelly. (Mother has just produced this.)
Mother: It's a jelly, yes. What colour's the jelly?
Sally: Red jelly.
Mother: A red jelly. Put it on the table, Sally. There's no room for the tea-pot. We'll have to put it on the floor, Sally. What's this?
Sally approximates "cake".
Mother: A cake.
Sally: Cake (distinctly). There, put it there.
Mother: You don't put cake on the floor. Put cake on the table. What's this?
Sally: What's that?

79

Mother: It's the bread.
Sally: It (sic) the bread.
Mother: The bread.
Sally: Knife.
Mother: Oh dear! It fell off the table. We'll have to get a bigger table. What's this? (producing another table).
Sally: Table.
Mother: A table.
Sally makes unintelligible remark.
Mother: What's this? It's a television.
Sally: Television.
Mother: Yes. You put it on the table.
Sally: On the table.
Mother: Yes. It goes on the television table, doesn't it?
Sally: Oh, white outside. (Presumably referring to the colour of the television set.)
Mother: Is it?
Sally: Brown (obviously again referring to the set).
Mother: Here's another chair. We'll move these. We'll put these away. And now a bedroom.

The next transcription is from a tape recording made when Sally's age was 3 years 8 months, i.e. two months later. She and her mother are using a cardboard base on which have been crayoned fields with a road and a river running through them. There is also a pond. The mother has an open box, full of farm toys, which she keeps on the floor beside her—out of Sally's sight. The microphone of the tape recorder was unobtrusively positioned after Sally's mother had involved her in creating a farm scene.

Mother: It's another cow.
Sally: In the field. (Articulated almost correctly.)
Mother: In the field. Yes. It's another cow. What colour is this cow?
Sally: White and blown (sic).
Mother: That's right.
Sally: Is that little cow? (Then two unintelligible phrases.)
Mother: Two cows, isn't it? Two cows.
Sally: Two cows for dinner. Bull?
Mother: What's the bull say?
Sally makes a noise.
Mother: He says m-m-moo.
Sally: M-m-moo.

Mother: Yes.

Sally: And the cows say moo.

Mother: And the cows say moo.

Sally: Yes.

Mother: And what colour is the bull?

Sally: Orange.

Mother: He's orange. Yes. We'll put him in the field. Put him in the same field as the cows. Sally, put him with the cows in the same field.

Sally: Yes (and does so).

Mother: Yes. Who's this?

Sally: Baby calf lying down.

Mother: It's lying down. Yes.

Sally: Put it in the next field.

Mother: Well, put it with the cows.

Sally: No.

Mother: No? All right.

Sally: Put it in that field.

Mother: Here's another baby calf.

Sally approximates "Another baby calf", then says, "Lie down same that one".

Mother: Yes. What colour is this one.

Sally: Black and white.

Mother: That's right.

Sally: (evidently holding the calf over the base). That field?

Mother: In that field.

Sally: Yes.

Mother: (producing a horse). Who's this?

Sally: Horsey.

Mother: The horsey. What colour is the horse?

Sally: Blown (sic).

Mother: A brown horse. Yes. He's going to trot down the road. (She makes it do so quite noisily.) Trot down the road, horse.

Sally: ... bull.

Mother: Here's a man to ride the horse.

Sally: Yes.

Mother: A man to ride the horse.

Sally: A man. (Puts man on horse.) There—(long drawn-out vowel).

Mother: Sit down, man. (Sally laughs.) Yes. Sit down, man. Yes. He's riding the horse.

Sally approximates "Riding the horse".

Mother: Yes, he's going for a ride on the horse. You make him go down the road.

Sally: (doing so): There—(again long drawn-out vowel).

Mother: Go down the road horse.

Sally: Sit there, man (very distinctly).

Mother: Sit there man.

Sally: I like baby horse.

Mother: Baby horse. Yes.

Sally: Baby horse.

Mother: He's got some white socks.

Sally: Yes, white socks.

Mother: White socks. How many white socks?

Sally: Two ear.

Mother: Those are his ears. There are its white socks. One, two, three, four.

Sally: Yes.

Mother: Four white socks.

Sally: Four white socks. Another one now (obviously seeing another toy in mother's hand).

Mother: Yes. Put it with the mummy horse. What's this?

Sally: That's donkey.

Mother: That's a donkey. Yes. What do donkeys say?

Sally: Wha(t)?

Mother: What do donkeys say? Ee-aw.

Sally: Ee-aw.

Mother: Ee-aw. That one's saying ee-aw. That's a donkey. The donkey is coloured ...

Sally: (breaking in). In that one?

Mother: In that field. Yes. It's coloured grey.

Sally: Grey.

Mother: It's a grey donkey.

Sally: Is it?

Mother: Put it in the field.

Sally says "Yes" and does so.

Mother produces a sheep.

Sally: Sheep.

Mother: Yes. What colour is the sheep?

Sally: A black sheep.

Mother: It's got a black face but it's grey, isn't it?

Sally: Grey.

Mother: It's a grey sheep. Yes.

Sally: A grey sheep.

Mother: Put it in the field. Here's another sheep.

Sally: Another sheep.

Mother: What colour's this sheep?

Sally: It's grey.

Mother: Grey, with a black face, isn't it?

Sally: Black face.

Mother produces a lamb.

Sally: Baa-lamb.

Mother: Baa-lamb. Yes. What colour's the baa-lamb?

Sally: White.

Mother: A white baa-lamb.

Sally: Put in this field. Here, in here. (She puts the lamb down but it falls over.) Lying down baa-lamb. Fall, fall down.

Mother: Oh dear, it's fallen down.

Sally: Yes.

Mother: What's *this* baa-lamb doing?

Sally: Lying down.

Mother: And what's *this* baa-lamb doing?

Sally: Up.

Mother: It's standing up.

Sally's next utterance is unintelligible.

Mother: (Making the lamb jump on the table.) What's this baa-lamb doing now? What's the baa-lamb doing now? It's jumping. Look, it's jumping.

Sally: Yes.

5

Teaching deaf underfives, at school, to talk

Before detailing methods of teaching it is important to discuss the age at which hearing-impaired children should go to school. There is the unavoidable, background fact that, with the exception of those cases in which the handicap can be alleviated by medicine or surgery, the children will have to grow up with it and that it will stay with them for the whole of their lives. To help them to develop from their earliest age the special skills that will best fit them to meet their problems and needs is the prime objective. For all children, it is increasingly emphasised by many authorities that the first five years of life are crucial.

In a manual for parents of unhandicapped children, recently published, with the title *How to Raise a Brighter Child*, Mrs. Joan Beck, herself a mother of two, states that the prime rule is for parents to talk with their children as much as possible and to give the fullest possible answers to their questions. She has written "They cheer on his efforts to say the correct words, respond to him when he tries and when he succeeds, read to him and provide him with what experts call 'corrective feedback'. In this kind of rich, verbal environment a child's vocabulary grows, and his ability to use sentences develops. As he becomes more skilled with words, he learns to put his emotions and intentions into language. He begins to compare and to differentiate and to express abstract ideas. He uses words as tools of thought."

Our readers will have realised that these key principles of Mrs. Beck's manual for parents of unhandicapped children are the same as our experience has proved essential for the parents of the hearing impaired. They are principles that can be adequately applied with any underfives if a very considerable amount of individual attention is given to every child. How best to provide this for each child at home, in a play group, or at school and at what age, that is the question.

It is our experience that many severely and profoundly deaf children, for the purpose of learning to talk intelligibly, need more than home training can give them, by the age of three and a half or four years. Fully trained and qualified teachers of the deaf alone can fulfil their complicated needs. This particularly applies to children who are already home-trained and have begun to talk but whose auditory functioning has not, so far at any rate, indicated that they can learn to articulate correctly without expert help. In modern schools for the deaf hearing aid equipment and sound treatment of buildings provide facilities for developing to the full each child's hearing potential. The teachers' work is full-time to an extent that very few mothers can manage. Part of this chapter deals with more advanced methods than we include in parent guidance. Also, even parents who have been most dedicated in giving home training to their children have found that there has been a limit to the period of time over which they could sustain the main responsibility for their children's learning. Of course there is no question of parents ceasing to give skilled and careful help to their children after admission to school. The most successfully educated deaf children whom we have known have been given practical support by their parents right through their school lives and even afterwards. Parents should co-operate at all stages with their own children's class teachers and accept and follow the advice and guidance that they so willingly give.

Provision of schooling for partially deaf or hard of hearing children varies in different countries or even in different areas of the same country. Age of admission also varies. Under some national and local authorities nursery classes for the hard of hearing are part of special schools or units. Elsewhere, parents have to rely solely on home training for such children. For them part-time attendance at play groups offers a wider range of activities than most parents can provide at home. For guidance about the needs of hearing-impaired children and understanding of their handicap staff members have to rely on visiting teachers of the deaf and on the parents. In this situation, individual attention to development of spoken language through continued daily home training is indispensable. In a play group, most of the time, there is too much noise for hard of hearing children to get much benefit from hearing aids.

In play groups, staff members meet an important need of hard of hearing children when they encourage unhandicapped children to play with them. Solitary play has, of course, its place but in situations in which it is natural for underfives to be associated with each other it is only too easy for a hearing-impaired child to be left out or to keep out. Even before the age of five the unhandicapped can learn to imitate staff members as to the way in which they talk so as to make it possible for the hard of hearing to lipread. In our experience it is over-optimistic to suppose that children with defective hearing are encouraged to learn to talk simply as a result of the presence of children with normal hearing.

It is probably true that for a majority of hard of hearing underfives neither play groups nor nursery classes are as yet available. Home training by their parents, under guidance, may well be their sole source of help. Without that, as results of our tests of children in ordinary schools, found to be hard of hearing, have shown, they can be seriously retarded in ability to use and understand spoken language and also socially, in general knowledge and progress at school. Clearly, these facts stress the urgency of screening tests of hearing for underfives, of universal audiology clinics and of expert guidance for parents of all hearing-impaired children. It is particularly the case that in early childhood partial deafness can so easily be missed.

Should deaf children ever go to school before the age of three years? We believe that this should only be in exceptional circumstances. We have seen mothers who were unable to cope because of continual ill health, with no relative or other woman available to help them during frequent or prolonged illness. Even in the Western world there are still deaf children, unfortunately, with dire poverty in their homes. There are exceptional cases of very incompetent home management. There are mothers who are obliged to go out to work to support themselves and their children because of broken homes or when they are unmarried. It is impracticable for deaf parents who themselves cannot talk to give their children home training of a kind described in this book.

Geography usually dictates whether any deaf child should be admitted as a day pupil or a boarding pupil. There is a narrow limit to the distance which it is good for a little child to travel each day. This factor also affects the practicability of parents taking boarding pupils home each weekend.

A child entered as a day pupil has the obvious advantage of living in his own home, in daily contact with his parents, and of growing up with any brothers or sisters.

Besides the parents unable to benefit from guidance about the home training of their children there are still in most if not all countries many parents for whom guidance is not available, with the exception of those who can use a correspondence course. If, by the age of three and a half years, there has been no communication by spoken language between parents and child there is no effective parent–child relationship. Usually, there is much frustration on both sides. Essentially, a nursery class for deaf children must begin to compensate for this deprivation by providing a talking environment.

As in home training, obvious objectives are development of co-operative play, as a means of contriving occasions for adult–child communication, speech readiness and articulation readiness. Often, in a nursery class, or reception class, an individual child's free play can be utilised by the expert as an opportunity to come in and, with pleasure and satisfaction to the child, convert it to co-operative play. A wider range of play material, including larger items, than can usually be made available in a private home, is possible in a nursery classroom. For instance, a child may be enjoying himself in a Wendy (play) house. Say he is busy with a baby and a bed. The teacher contrives to catch his glance and quickly says "You're putting the baby to bed," or "You're getting baby up." Useful follow-ups may be "Let's tuck baby up", "Go to sleep baby (patting it)" or "Let's put baby's frock on. Isn't it pretty! " "Now let's brush baby's hair." The child may be sweeping the floor of the play house. Using the same technique the teacher says "Oh, you're sweeping the floor." She might then produce a dust-pan and say "Here's the dust-pan. You sweep the dust into the dust-pan" and, stooping down, holds out the pan to the child.

As with all beginning pupils in a school for the deaf the teacher needs to contrive opportunities, directly related to a succession of actions, of using the same words in similar phrases. Next, for instance, she may say, holding the dust-pan, "You swept the dust into the dust-pan." In our experience underfive boys enjoy and choose domestic play just as much as underfive girls.

Not breaking for too long into each pupil's free play, the teacher moves from child to child utilising each one's chosen activity. This method, of course, can be applied not only in the classroom, but also in the playroom or playground.

Very likely the teacher has a nursery aide whom she trains in play-talk techniques. When she has this help, and in England it is provided in most, if not all, nursery schools for the deaf, she is able to give every child at least one short daily period individually with a speech and auditory training broadband amplifier. The same methods of co-operative play that have been described in the previous chapter on home training have proved most effective.

Toys in a nursery class for deaf children, like those for home training, even those to be used for free play, need to be carefully selected. The reason for this is that they have to be toys that promote opportunities for co-operation, conversation and the learning by the children of new vocabulary and new language forms. For instance, a toy garage with different types of motor vehicles offers facilities for such actions and verbalisations of them as "Push the truck to the petrol pump", "Where shall we make the lady walk?" "You made the lady walk to the car", "Push the car up the ramp", "Make the man run to the ambulance", "You pushed the tanker to the pump", "Oh, the man ran to the ambulance very fast", "Where will you push the tanker?". Toy tea sets offer a good many possibilities. "Be careful, the teapot's hot", "What shall we put in the cup?", "Oh, you poured some milk into the cup", "What will you pour out now?", "How do we stir the tea?" "Ask the dolly if she wants more tea", "Oh dear, I've spilt the tea. What a mess!", "Would you like some bread or some cake?" (teacher holding toy bread in one hand and toy cake in the other). The way in which a child answers questions and the amount of prompting that he needs will depend on the stage that he has reached in learning to talk.

Of course, in nurseries for non-deaf children much importance is given to toys that stimulate large movements. These include kiddy cars, tricycles, slides, climbing frames and so on. Deaf children need them too. It is advisable to arrange that they be used in playrooms external to the teaching rooms and out of doors. Such toys offer little or no opportunity for conversation, new vocabulary and sentence structures which we firmly believe to be the primary need of deaf children.

Long experience of entrants who had been successfully home-trained emphasised the importance of organising and teaching them in groups separate from the entrants who had had no home training. The successfully home-trained children had begun to talk or at least had achieved speech readiness before coming to school. They were ready to progress more quickly, with use of larger vocabularies and longer and more varied sentence structures. They were already accustomed to periods at a play-table with an adult using a speech and auditory training unit. All this rendered them a very definite stage in advance of the non-home-trained with whom the initial aim was to develop speech readiness, primarily speech reception, ahead of expressive use of spoken language. We are convinced that no formal teaching in articulation ought to be given before children have reached that stage. The home-trained are ready for more advanced teaching when they have begun to talk spontaneously. In that case the motivation is already there. For the non-home-trained it has still to be developed.

It is best to make the introduction of group lessons a gradual process. For instance, the teacher will attract, perhaps, to start with, two children to join in making dough with flour and water. Other children notice what is happening and spontaneously come to take part. This gives plenty of opportunity to develop children's understanding of such sentences as "Here's some flour—Here's a bowl—Bobby, you put the flour into the bowl (he does so)—Oh, what have I got here? (showing a jug of water)—Yes, it's a jug of water (providing corrective feedback to a child's attempt)—Where shall we pour the water?—Yes, into the bowl (again corrective feedback)—Sheila, pour the water into the bowl—What did Sheila do?—Yes, she poured the water into the bowl—What's this?—Yes, it's a spoon. Tom, you stir the flour and water—That's right. What did Tom do?" etc.

The teacher chooses a different child for each of the actions. When the dough has been made it can be rolled out and cut into shapes, using the same teaching techniques, or else each child can be given a share of the dough to make whatever he chooses.

A subject that has proved attractive to little deaf children is making a home for a goldfish. To suit underfives this can be made

7

very simple. When the teacher puts on the table a glass jar with a live goldfish in it children are sure to gather round. The method of the lesson may be as follows:

Teacher (holding up the jar): What's this?

Children: Fish.

Teacher: Yes, it's a *gold*fish. What is the goldfish doing? It's swimming. What is the goldfish doing?

Children probably attempt "swimming".

Teacher: (corrective feedback). Yes, it's swimming—The jar is very small. Poor goldfish. What's this? (Producing a big bowl or tank.)

Children: A bowl.

Teacher: Yes, it's a *big* bowl. What shall we put into the bowl?

Children: Water.

Teacher: Yes, water. But wait a minute! (Producing some little pebbles.) Here are some pebbles to put in the bowl. These are pebbles. You feel them. (She lets the children handle them, particularly if it's a new word and a new concept for them.) Tom, put the pebbles in the bowl—What did Tom do?

Children: answer, perhaps with incomplete sentences, like "Tom peb in bowl".

Teacher: Yes, Tom put *the pebbles* in the bowl. Now we'll have the water. Where is it? (Pretending to look about for it.)

Children: There (or perhaps) Over there.

Teacher: Oh, there it is! Mary, come and get the water. That's right. What's Mary going to do with the water?

Children: Water OR Bowl OR Put in bowl OR Pour in bowl.

Teacher: Yes, she's going to pour the water into the bowl.

Mary does so.

Teacher: Mary poured the water into the bowl. Now what shall we put in the water?

Children: Fish OR Goldfish.

Teacher: Yes, the goldfish. (She picks up the goldfish and herself transfers it into the bowl.) Where's the goldfish?

Children: In the bowl OR Bowl OR In the water.

Teacher: Yes, the goldfish is in the bowl. Look, the goldfish is swimming.

If the children are sufficiently interested and still concentrating their attention on the activity the teacher may continue this group lesson by introducing food for the goldfish.

Throughout all group lessons the intention of which is to develop communication the teacher is training the children in a special combination of habits that will be important to them through life. She wants them to become keenly interested in what is happening and being done by them. Also, she wants them to develop a habit, during such lessons as these, of being in continuous contact with her so that they keep looking up to lipread what she says, to back up whatever they manage to hear with their aids. Her skill in use of microphone techniques, which we discuss in the next chapter of this book, may also be important. Once the children have begun to join in group lessons, introduction of an inductance system can be made to minimise the disadvantages resulting from varying distances between the children's hearing aids and the teacher's lips. With this apparatus every child hears the teacher's speech as picked up by a microphone which she wears or holds.

Like all children when learning to talk and to use their native language, deaf children need to have very much practice in learning to verbalise what they are doing. During a group lesson, this is extended to include verbalisation of what other children and the teacher are doing. To a greater or lesser extent for most deaf children auditory feedback—hearing themselves talk—stimulates motivation and helps them in control of their own speech. Here again, microphone techniques enter the picture. To hear and see a profoundly deaf child, playing alone, begin to verbalise to herself entirely spontaneously has been, indeed, a thrilling experience!

As soon as deaf children have begun to understand spoken language and to talk and have started to enjoy group activities they can be proved ready to obtain fun and pleasure from simple stories. These are best told very freely and informally, with no restriction to a prescribed vocabulary. Things are made to happen. What is needed is a great variety of real-life objects and toys, representing people and things that the children may meet. These serve a dual purpose. They facilitate the children's speech reception by providing a concrete context. Equally important, they are things that the children can move about, acting out with their help successive incidents in a story. And, of course, one is testing the accuracy with which a child has understood what has been said by finding if he can do the right thing.

An initiatory story for little deaf children can be made to centre round a doll that is taken for a walk in a pram, falls out and is picked up by a dog which runs away with it. The method might well be as follows: unknown to the children, the teacher, before beginning the story will have placed the necessary toys or models in different parts of the room where the children will easily be able to find them. She will also have prepared pictures to illustrate some of the episodes but will not show any picture until the relevant episode has been acted out by children. This is so that, step by step, the children will rely on the spoken word as a basis for following the story. When they are introduced they confirm the children in their understanding of the story. They also accustom the children to a temporal sequence of events.

Teacher: Once upon a time there was a little girl. (Then, looking around.) Where's a little girl? Yes. you're girls. This little girl had a pram. (Then again looking round.) Can you find a pram? Mary, can you find a pram? That's right. Bring it over here. (Mary does so and sits down. Teacher, touching the pram, asks) What's this? (This is to encourage speech from the children.)

Teacher, continuing: The little girl put a doll in the pram. Joan, you fetch a doll. (To the group) What's this? Yes, it's a doll. Joan, put it in the pram. (Joan does so and sits down.) The little girl went for a walk. She pushed the pram. Susan, you come and push the pram. (Susan having done so, this is a good opportunity for the teacher to produce the first picture. It shows a little girl pushing a pram with a doll in it.) Teacher, pointing successively to the girl, the pram and the doll: What's this? What's the girl doing? Yes, she's pushing the pram. (Continuing the story.) Oh dear! (With suitable expression.) The doll fell out! Bobby, you make the doll fall out. Oh dear! You say "Oh dear!" (Encouraging them all to do so loudly.)

Teacher: A big dog came. It was a very big dog. Jimmy, where is a dog? Yes, that's a dog. Bring it here. It's a very small dog, it's too small. Jimmy, you be a big dog. (Showing him how to get down on all fours and be a dog. Then, to make sure that the group understands the pretence.) What's this? Yes, it's a big dog. Oh, what do dogs say? (Children pretend to bark, noisily.)

Teacher: The dog ran and picked up the doll in his mouth. (To Jimmy) Pick up the doll. The dog ran away. It ran away very fast. (Jimmy did so.) The little girl cried. (To group): You cry. Oo, what a noise! (With facial expression suitable to encourage loudness.) Jennifer, go to the pram and cry.

The teacher now produces a picture of an empty pram. The little girl standing by it and crying and a dog running away with the doll. She recapitulates what it illustrates. During this time Jimmy continues to hold the doll.

Teacher: A little boy ran to the dog. Paul, you be the boy and run to the dog. The boy caught the dog. Paul, catch the dog. The boy took the doll away from the dog. He ran to the little girl. (The teacher will have arranged that a little girl is standing by the pram crying.) The boy gave the doll to the girl. The little girl said "Thank you." She put the doll in the pram.

The teacher now produces the third picture showing the little girl putting the doll back in the pram, the boy watching and the dog in the distance.

We hope that this last story makes clear certain key points about our method. First, that with underfives, the teacher chiefly uses vocabulary already known to the group as a whole. In the way in which she tells the story she ensures a number of repetitions of particular words and phrases. She involves as many children as possible as actors. She encourages them to participate imaginatively by identifying themselves with characters in the story. As children become more accustomed to this kind of story-telling the teacher brings in more dialogue between the characters. This is to encourage use of spoken language between the children themselves apart from lessons.

All kinds of stories, suitable to children's ages, and factual lessons too, prepare them for the beginnings of reading. There can, of course, be no question about the value to deaf children of learning to read. The printed or the written version of a word or phrase is often, for many of them, more complete than the version that they can obtain from amplified hearing combined with lip-reading. A child can look twice, or several times, at what is written or in print, by contrast with the very quick, transitory nature of spoken language. On the other hand the patterning of written and printed language is very complicated from a child's point of view, as well as being less personal. Unhandicapped children are not normally thought of as mature enough to learn to read until long after they have learnt to talk. Here we would stress that for deaf children, as for the unhandicapped, we have found that they learn more quickly and more meaningfully to read when they have a good basis of spoken language. For that reason, we are not including in this book about underfives any suggestions as to the age and stage at which children should first be taught to read. Informally, a little experience of reading is inevitably offered to some young pupils in school. They see their own names and those of other children in the cloak-rooms, by the pegs for their hats and coats. Their names are written on paintings and drawings and often on their personal possessions. At boarding school children receive letters and begin to learn to pick out words, e.g. "Mummy", as the letters are read to them by an adult. In many children's picture books they see words printed below or by pictures. Such experiences as these can be made a useful first step towards reading readiness without any risk of undermining a deaf child's developing reliance on spoken language as the basis of communication and verbal thinking. This is not to say that there are no circumstances in which children under five who are deaf should be taught to read.

With numbers, as with reading, an informal and incidental type of approach has proved useful for the underfives. Playfully, an adult will show a child how to count the few buttons on his coat, comparing them, perhaps, with the number on another child's coat. With a group who have become involved in co-operative play-talk with, say, a toy teaset, the number of children is counted and compared with the number of cups, saucers and plates. A young child can learn to take a specified number of sweets. When threading beads of two different colours, he is encouraged to make patterns, alternating, say, two red with two green. In all cases, of course, the purpose is to help a child to develop concepts of different numbers by learning to apply them to little groups of different kinds of objects.

To create and provide a talking environment out of school is just as important as in the classrooms. In a day school or in a public day class this is primarily the responsibility of parents. Most parents are willing and anxious to co-operate with staff. This in itself straightway indicates a necessity for a continuing and progressive form of guiding lines to parents of hearing-impaired children until they leave school.

At a boarding school the main responsibility belongs to the staff although guidance to parents is of very great importance indeed, even if it can only be given by post. It has proved immensely advantageous to train the house-mothers and their assistants to talk suitably to the children and to give them every encouragement to talk, from getting up in the morning until going to bed, in the playground, at meal times, when dressing and bathing. For a teacher to be on duty, moving from house to house and group to group, is a great help to both children and house staff.

There are a number of key factors of which house-mothers and their helpers need to be aware and which are crucial to the valuable help that they can give to deaf underfives in learning to talk. First there is the skill that is needed to make it as easy as possible for the children to lipread. As for the parents and teachers, this involves positioning oneself, whenever possible, with one's face in a good light, on a level with the child's—bending down, kneeling or sitting on a low chair. A good instance is that of putting on a little child's coat. Having helped the child to insert his arms into the sleeves, one kneels in front and catching the child's eye, as one does up the buttons, one says "You've put your coat on. Here are the buttons, one, two, three. . . ." Rate and distinctness of speaking matter a great deal. So does facial expression. The method just described applies equally to effectiveness of the children's use of their hearing aids just as much as to lipreading. Speech should be neither too quick nor too slow. A clear, steady voice is needed to enable the hearing aids to work at their maximum efficiency.

Through each child's teacher, house-mothers and their staff need to keep familiar with his progress in the classroom, in learning to understand spoken language and to talk, in order that they may encourage free use of voice and attempts to talk out of school. It has been proved valuable in several countries for house-mothers and their assistants to have periods of observation in classrooms. Besides other things, this enables them to learn how the teachers relate development of the children's spoken language to cooperative play and how they make use of practical situations.

As all this implies, house staffs, and parents too, cannot adequately meet deaf children's needs without having enough time to do so. This in turn, in a boarding school, necessitates a generous staff–pupil ratio.

A major need in the education of all deaf children is to find ways of helping them to become able to talk intelligibly. For very many children, unhandicapped as well as hearing-impaired, there tend to be two stages. At first, what they say or are trying to say is understood much better by parents and others who have had time to get used to their incomplete articulation. At this stage someone who has not had opportunity to become accustomed to it often has much greater difficulty. The second stage of speaking clearly

95

enough to be understood by anyone who uses the same language is ordinarily reached by unhandicapped children before they are five years old. This poses a problem for teachers of the deaf whose pupils' progress in learning to talk has begun later and inevitably tends to take place more slowly. By the age of five it is of the utmost importance for them also to be on the way to clear speech. By the age of five, failure to make themselves understood is liable to cause frustration. The children themselves and their parents can begin to be aware of the handicap as a socially separating factor. This operates in direct opposition to the process of integration. For the children to have reached the first stage of being able to make themselves understood, through speech, by people who are used to them, is a great step in the right direction.

The first requisite for all deaf children when learning to talk is to form a habit of using audible voices. More than that, they need, if possible, to vary intonation in the way to which ordinary listeners are accustomed and which helps to convey meaning.

What is called the ear to voice link is the most natural physiological basis for use of voice. We learn to talk not only by hearing other people do so but also by hearing our own voices—ourselves speaking. Quite unconsciously, in ordinary circumstances we learn to match our own utterances to those of our social environment. Unhandicapped infants before beginning to talk can be heard enjoying the sound of their own voices as they babble to themselves for quite appreciable periods of time.

Many deaf children cannot hear any sound of their own voices without amplification, in some cases even if they shout. For them, initial establishment of an ear to voice link is usually dependent on training by skilled adults using suitable hearing aid equipment. In most cases a hearing and speech training aid is indispensable. For underfives at school the same principles are applicable as those to which we referred briefly in Chapter Four. Two essential features of the relevant methods are: (a) provision for the child as well as the adult to speak at a distance of not more than four to six inches from a microphone of the hearing aid (with a form of amplification that is not easily overloaded) and (b) for training that is directed towards the specific objective of giving the child experience and practice in hearing his own voice while he uses it. The technological considerations of this are outlined in Chapter Six.

As yet, many deaf children enter school without having had home training and without any functioning of an ear to voice link. For them, as in home training, development of a happy relationship between child and adult is the first prerequisite so that he comes to feel that anything which she provides is interesting and pleasurable. As soon as the teacher has enabled a child to discover the pleasure of co-operative play he can be attracted to the play table with a toy that he has not seen before. This should be a noise-making toy. Xylophones, particularly larger ones producing resonant musical tones, do very well. This is because the child can see movement that produces sound which, in most cases, if suitably amplified, he can become able to hear and also because he can feel and see himself imitate the movements shown to him by his teacher.

A good many underfives, we have found, once attracted to a xylophone or other noisemaker will accept without difficulty the wearing of a headset of a training hearing aid or speech trainer. Other children demur. With them the point is first to make sure that they are visually attracted to the xylophone as they or the teacher play it. Once this has begun the teacher unobtrusively holds one of the receivers of the headset fairly close to the child's ear but without touching it. For the time being the receiver is being used as a loud speaker so that the child may experience sound, perhaps without being aware of the fact, whenever the teacher or he plays the instrument. Gradually, the earphone is moved closer and closer to the child's ear, so increasing the strength of the available sound, and finally it is brought in contact with the ear. More often than not the child by now discovers sound as something that he can enjoy making. Once he has accepted the positioning of a receiver on his ear he will usually be willing to wear the headset with both receivers.

Volume settings of the training hearing aid are, of course, important. If an audiogram or results of calibrated free-field testing are available our own practice is to begin by setting attenuators or volume controls to give amplification ten decibels above the threshold level for each of the child's ears. When a child has become accustomed to the headset and seems happy about listening we try giving him a further ten decibels amplification, looking for any evidence as to whether or not he seems to hear better as a result.

97

If no quantitative results have been supplied as part of the child's history when admitted to a special school or class and no facilities for obtaining such results are available within the school, referral to the nearest audiologist is necessary before auditory training with the school equipment is begun.

Quite a good way to begin use of the training hearing aid is for the teacher to take the xylophone to the child, wherever in the room he is. She shows it to him and says "Look at this lovely xylophone! Come with me and we'll play it." Besides attracting the child to the instrument this helps to persuade him to sit at the play-table near the speech training aid. We have never used force to compel a child to comply in this or any similar situation.

Both being seated, the teacher says "Here's a hammer", holding it, of course, close to her face. "I'll play the xylophone." She plays a lively tune, expressing great enjoyment as she does so. Then to involve the child more fully she produces a second hammer, saying "Here's a hammer for you. You play the xylophone," and gives it to him. While both are playing the xylophone, the teacher uses her spare hand to begin the use of the headset, following, if necessary, the plan that has been described above. We suggest that both together should play the xylophone because so often a deaf child, in his first attempt, fails to produce sound that is loud enough for him to have a chance of hearing it, even through the earphones.

Once the headset is accepted and the volume controls adjusted the child is ready to be given experience of voice through the training aid with the object, of course, of bringing it about that he hears his own voice. A good method has proved to be for the teacher to let him see and hear her singing "ba baba, baba", etc. in time with the lively tune that she is playing on the xylophone. The syllable "ba" is chosen because the labial consonant and the mouth movement as a whole are much more visible than in "la-lala lala" and, therefore, much more likely to achieve the desired end of stimulating the child to imitate the teacher and thus hear his own voice.

Besides showing pleasure when the child uses his voice the situation makes a good opportunity for the teacher, by saying to him "That's a pretty voice", to begin to build up in his mind a concept of it. Presently, if the child speaks voicelessly, he will understand what the teacher means and respond correctly when she says "Where's that pretty voice?" This is particularly helpful when a child is using his bodyworn aid and when it does not give him a really effective ear to voice link.

There are other noisemakers that can be used in such a way as to stimulate a child's vocalisation during sessions with the speech training aid. Here are a few suggestions. A toy car is held by the teacher as she pushes it across the play-table towards the child saying "brr" in time with its movement. The child is encouraged to imitate the same action and to make the same vocal sound. A railway engine with an accompanying "bumpity bumpity" by the teacher can fulfil a similar purpose. Farm animals can be made equally effective and a variety of vowel sounds can be related to them—BAA with the sheep, MOO with the cow, HEE-HAW with the donkey, MIAOW with the cat and so on.

The extent to which the ear to voice link promotes distinct speech varies greatly among young deaf children of similar ages. With all, except a few totally deaf, it establishes some degree of natural physiological basis. As regards auditory discrimination, hearing and speech sessions at the play-table with the training aid provide the best facilities for developing each child's potential. Audiograms, with medical histories that report the pathology of deafness, afford very useful indications. With many deaf under-fives, however, potential for auditory discrimination can only be adequately ascertained through a considerable amount of the special training. We have quoted in detail, earlier in this book, actual results with a number of home trained children.

There is no avoiding the fact that there are cases of very severe, profound or even total deafness in which the hearing-lipreading method does not afford a child enough cues to promote good all-round articulation. Even with the training aid he does not hear his teacher or himself sufficiently distinctly. We have proved this by tests of older pupils in the primary stage.

Articulation readiness is a term that we have used in previous books. It indicates adopting methods of developing in deaf under-fives perception and use of articulatory patterns unavailable or only imperfectly available to them through amplified hearing and lipreading. The methods in question provide reinforcement in cases in which the patterns are partially heard and partially visible. They have proved successful with many underfives not yet mature enough for formal teaching. In a nursery class the methods can be followed contemporaneously with the play-talk method—indeed they are carried out in the same sort of way.

It is best to begin during periods of individual play-talk with a speech and auditory training hearing aid. As usual teacher and child are facing each other across the play table. The game is one in which the child is learning with amusement to make certain types of movements or shapes, some of them with his hand or fingers, also to understand his teacher's verbal description of them. Initially, he is not made aware that the objective of the game is to help him to talk distinctly. At a later stage, when he is mature enough and can produce a particular pattern of movement in response to his teacher's spoken description of it, it can be directly applied to his utterance of particular words and phrases when they need improvement.

One of the simplest examples of the introductory training that has proved so useful to many little deaf children teaches the concept and habit of FLICK. A FLICK is, of course, an outstanding characteristic of plosive consonants. Of these /p/, /t/ and /k/, because they are unvoiced, are not likely to be clearly heard by very many severely deaf children either by their own "envelopes" of sound or as regards their modification of abutting vowels.

The teacher produces a ping-pong ball. This is small and light. Brightly coloured ones are obtainable. The teacher says "Here's a little ball. I'll flick it to you." She does so, with a sharp movement of forefinger and thumb of one hand. She asks the child, who now has the ball, to "Flick the ball to me". This is repeated several times. Little toys that will rock when flicked make another game.

By contrast, playing with a ping-pong ball in a different way can prepare a child for learning later the articulatory patterns of continuant unvoiced consonants inclusive of /f/, /th/, /s/, /sh/. One of the outstanding characteristics is an uninterrupted FLOW of breath. In normal, continuous speech the duration of these consonants is very brief. For deaf children to learn the relevant concepts and habits, experience of sensation with longer duration is inevitably necessary.

The teacher says "Now we're going to make the ball FLOW". She demonstrates how a ping-pong ball can be made to roll slowly, perhaps between goal-posts, by blowing it with a steady controlled flow of breath. She says to the child "Now you blow slowly and make the ball flow." This little game can be repeated several times on different occasions.

There are some underfives who, having learnt the habits and concepts of FLICK and FLOW, are ready to go further. They are described as articulation ready. As an example, such a child, when he says "boa'" for "boat", can be reminded of the word FLICK. He's asked to flick with his finger and thumb. After he has done that efficiently his teacher says to him, "Now I'm going to flick with my tongue". With the child watching her, she flicks with her finger near her mouth at the moment when she articulates clearly the /t/ in "boat". Next she says "Now you make a flick and say "boat". Very soon, when the child omits to articulate a /t/ in any word in which he is thought capable of using one, it will be enough for his teacher to remind him of it—"Where's that flick?" Of course, this applies to words having an initial or medial /t/ as well as to those with a final /t/. Further stages in the application of this principle and method with children aged over five years, are described in our previous book, *Teaching Deaf Children to Talk*.

To draw attention, when a child has reached articulation readiness, to the flow of breath that he needs to produce as a key feature when articulating /f/ or /th/ (thin) is comparatively simple. The long-established practice of helping him to feel the flow on the back of his hand, held close to his mouth, offers a useful additional cue supplementing visual ones. In our experience the consonant /sh/ is one of those that young deaf children tend to identify and use with least difficulty. As articulated by most speakers /sh/ involves an obvious lip movement varying, in some degree, in relation to abutting vowels. For some deaf children there are auditory cues. Once again, a flow of breath is a key feature. This is true, also, of the consonant /s/ although the emission of breath is more faintly felt on the back of the hand. In normal continuous speech the consonant /s/ produces little or no visible movement. With many young deaf children, again after they have become articulation ready, it has proved helpful to teach them to direct the flow of breath along a narrow channel. The teacher shows the child how one can shape the fingers and palm of one's hand to make a channel, extending from the fingertips to the wrist. Using his hand to provide the channel, she lets him feel the flow of her breath as she produces a prolonged /s/.

101

He is asked to make his own breath flow to give a similar effect. He sees that though her lips are parted her mouth is not open. The success with this method is apparently due to its producing in the child an unconscious reaction involving an appropriately channelled type of tongue movement.

Some simple play methods that help towards preparing severely deaf underfives in distinct vowel articulation centre round learning to make specific shapes. Plasticine is a good medium—soft, easily moulded and it can be attractive in colour. An attractive little game is making a cradle or hollow for a tiny baby doll. The teacher, producing the little doll, says "Let's make a cradle for the baby" and on this first occasion shows the child how to do it. She gives the child some plasticine and says "You make a cradle for the baby." To ensure the child is learning both the shape and the meaning of the word, the teacher, on later occasions on which the child is playing with plasticine, suggests to him that he makes a cradle for a baby, perhaps models a plasticine baby to put in a cradle. Another time, the teacher will say "Make a cradle for the baby with your hand." The intention of these kinds of play is, of course, to prepare a deaf child with limited potential for auditory discrimination to articulate the vowel /ah/ as pronounced by many English-speaking people in words like CAR, FARM, LAUGH, BATH. Here hollowing the tongue is a key feature. We have found that quite young deaf children easily and without conscious control of the tongue—the object of these analogies—reproduce with it the cradle shape that they have become accustomed, automatically, to make with their hand at the teacher's verbal request.

The English vowels /oo/ and /aw/ and diphthongs /oh/ and /ow/ tend to involve some degree of rounding and protrusion of the lips. Perhaps it is for this reason that many young deaf children learn to articulate them as a result of direct imitation, even though their capacity for auditory discrimination is limited. Other children, including some who are dysphasic, are helped by methods that draw conscious attention to form and movement. A preparatory approach to the concept of ROUND can be made in play form, e.g. by making wheels in plasticine. Four-year-olds can cut them out in paper. The teacher, of course, will say "You've made a ROUND wheel." Later, if occasion arises, and the children mispronounce the vowel in TWO or SHOE they can be asked to "make it round".

On the same principle play activities like PRESSING wheels on a car, PRESSING shapes out of dough or plasticine or coloured adhesive shapes on paper can establish a useful foundation for teaching a child later on to exert somewhat greater pressure with his tongue in articulating "ee" or "n".

We have not found it advisable or helpful, with severely deaf children under five, to begin any articulation teaching other than that which can be easily related to play activities. It is on this basis that children can learn to enjoy speech improvement.

6

Clinic tests and hearing aids

First and foremost, this chapter is intended to help parents to understand and think over results of clinic tests of their children's hearing. How far do these results indicate what a child can hear (a) without a hearing aid and (b) with hearing aids of different kinds? We try to explain the subject only and specially as it relates to hearing-impaired children under five years of age. To find scientific answers to the relevant questions is one part of an audiologist's task. He has also to provide as much data as possible that will be helpful to medical diagnosis, but that part of the subject will not be discussed in this chapter except in so far as it also concerns a child's dependence on his hearing in learning to talk.

Figure 1 illustrates in a much simplified way some of the key facts about the pitch and loudness levels of speech, expanding information already given in Chapters Two and Three.

The figures along the horizontal line at the top of the diagram can be thought of as representing something like a piano keyboard. A big difference is immediately noticeable. The frequency (pitch) of 250 vibrations per second (0.25 K.Hz or 250 hertz)[1] is the scientific round-figure equivalent of middle C on the piano. The shaded part of the diagram shows the range of frequency and intensity (loudness) of the actual sound of speech at conversational level when scientifically measured. It is at once clear that by far the greater part of the sound that we need to be able to hear, if we are not to miss some of the important sound patternings of speech, extends to five octaves above 250 vibrations per second (middle C). This is a very wide range indeed. This is

[1] 1 K.Hz—one kilohertz = 1,000 vibrations per second = one kilocycle.

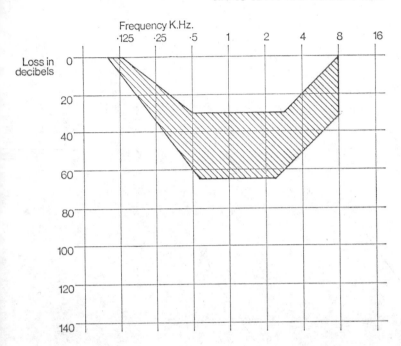

 65 db speech

FIG. 1. Pure-tone audiogram: speech area

brought home to us if we think for a moment of the contrast
between the notes that a man with a deep bass voice can sing or
with which he can talk, and the extremely high-pitched sound
that we can produce if we articulate an /s/, or a /th/ (thin), or
an /f/, separately from any words or vowels. In fact, most of the
sound that we make when articulating /s/ in a normal way in
connected speech is contained within the top octave of the speech
range. The consonants /f/ and /th/ (thin) both give very high-
pitched sound. Pioneer research by Dr. Harvey Fletcher and
others in Bell Telephone Laboratories, New York, showed long
ago that the clearness with which speech as a whole is heard
depends much more on the audibility of sound in the three upper
octaves of the speech range than on the audibility of it in the
lower three.

Occasionally even adult listeners with unimpaired hearing, in ordinary life conditions, have the experience of hearing a voice without being able to distinguish what is said—for instance, when listening to someone shouting in the distance. For many years we have played recordings of filtered speech to demonstrate this to audiences of parents, teachers, doctors, health visitors and others. At the beginning of the record one hears words reproduced with the highest degree of accuracy that very good equipment is capable of giving. The next list has been recorded through a filter that eliminates sound in the highest octave of the speech range of frequencies. Another list follows with sound over the two highest octaves cut out. At this point it is invariable for audiences to begin to have considerable difficulty. With more severe filtering the difficulty grows more acute. The point is heavily emphasised that deaf children learning to talk have to be enabled, if at all possible, to hear speech in the higher-pitched part of the range of the sound represented by the shaded part of our diagram.

This brings us to another essential point—the way in which the sound of speech varies very much in loudness. First, there is a wide difference between the loudness of particular vowels and consonants although a person is talking with an even voice. To give an example: the vowel /aw/ has more than a hundred times the intensity of the consonant /f/. There is another point here. Scientists prefer to use the term INTENSITY to describe the amount of physical energy possessed by a particular sound. Everyone, probably, is aware that the apparent loudness of a sound depends on its nature and the conditions in which we hear it. A sound that may seem very loud if we suddenly hear it in quiet conditions may be hardly noticeable against a continuous noisy background. For the same sort of reason the term FREQUENCY that we have already introduced above is preferred to the word pitch.

Perhaps one of the items of information that parents most wish to have is the meaning of their child's AUDIOGRAM. They see the headset fitted on his head, connected by a fairly thick cable to the large electronic instrument, called a pure-tone audiometer. If he is under five years of age they will have watched and heard him being given training to prepare him for the test, before the headset was fitted. The method is similar to that which we have described under Item 7 of the Screening Tests in Chapter Two. First the child is encouraged to insert a peg into a board or build

a tower with bricks, one at a time, as soon as he sees and hears a loud sound being made, probably the word "now", or "go". Then he learns to respond to the sound without watching for it. It is after the tester has made sure that the child knows that he must wait to hear the sound before moving the play object that the test proper begins.

Provided that a child is in the right state of attention and has been motivated to co-operate carefully in what should be presented to him as a kind of game, a pure-tone audiometer is a very accurate means for finding exactly what intensity sound has to reach for him just to be able to hear it. This means that the tester has to follow a prescribed procedure to find that level, which is called the THRESHOLD. The sounds that the audiometer produces are called PURE TONES because they are restricted to a single frequency.

Just to clarify the significance of being able to hear sound in the high frequency part of the speech range we quote results of testing Fiona. She was much less severely deaf than any underfive whose history has been given in this book. She would best be described as somewhat hard of hearing. An intelligent schoolgirl, seventeen years old, her spoken language was normal and her progress at school good. Her headmaster described her as "a very retiring, quiet, shy girl, who does not always seem to follow what is said to her". Her audiogram, Fig. 2, showed that in the middle of the speech range at 1 K.Hz her hearing was within normal limits but that listening to typical conversational speech she would hear very little in the two octaves above 2 K.Hz.

Because we needed to investigate the extent to which Fiona had difficulty in hearing spoken language we gave her tests with a SPEECH AUDIOMETER. For this, of course, she was sufficiently mature and gave every evidence of having normally developed discrimination for speech sounds. The apparatus reproduces phonetically balanced lists of one-syllable words recorded on a tape at an even level of loudness in a sound-proofed laboratory. Each ear is tested separately through a high-quality earphone. The electronic equipment enables the intensity of the words to be regulated accurately at selected levels on a decibel scale. The patient is asked to repeat aloud each word as he or she hears it. Fiona was tested in a sound-treated clinic thus eliminating any risk of interference by any kind of background noise.

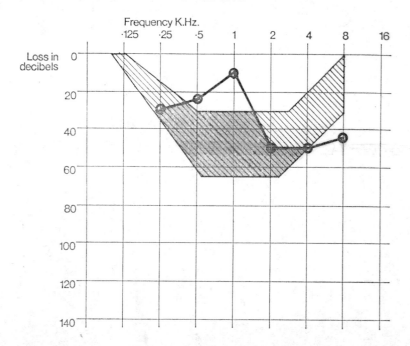

FIG. 2. Pure-tone audiogram of Fiona without hearing aid

Results of the speech audiometry showed that at a 60 decibel conversational level Fiona scored 75 per cent with the right ear and 65 per cent with the left. When the intensity level was lowered to 50 decibels her scores dropped to 45 per cent for the right ear and 50 per cent with the left. With only two exceptions, Fiona's mishearings were confined to consonants. Typical examples are: MOTH for MOSS, RAT for RAP, THUMB for FUN, RATE for RAKE, CATS for CATCH, HIVE for FIVE, DOT for GOT, FACE for FAITH, FINE for SIGN, BUS for BUFF, WAYS for WAVE, etc. These examples illustrate clearly how much ability to hear the sounds of consonants in speech accurately, especially those of unvoiced consonants, depends on ability to hear in the two upper frequencies

of the speech range. In Fiona's case, amplification could not be proved at the time of test to offer effective help towards overcoming her disability in real life situations. Facility for lipreading would be more effective.

Barry, a child less severely deaf than those quoted earlier in this book, was first seen in the Manchester University Clinic at the age of 3 years 8 months, when a sample audiogram at three frequencies was made. He was referred to a consultant otolaryngologist and the medical diagnosis was that of a mixed bilateral perceptive deafness. (This would indicate that there was an inner ear deficiency with a middle ear component.) Tonsils and adenoids were removed soon afterwards and later audiograms showed some improvement in hearing, although following the same pattern as the first one. A post-operative audiogram is given (Fig. 3).

Barry's audiogram differs from Fiona's. At no point in the speech range of frequencies above 0·125 K.Hz is auditory acuity in either ear shown to approach normal. A lesser area of typical conversational speech, as represented in the last diagram, is shown to be audible to him when listening with unaided hearing. Later tests showed his potential capacity to benefit from amplification to be very good. When first seen Barry was already talking freely in sentences. There were some deficiencies in his articulation and use of language. For instance, the consonant /s/ was usually omitted or mispronounced and sometimes /th/ (thin), e.g. "He blow(s) the whi(s)tle", "tweet" for sweet. During home training he had to be helped to learn prepositions and their use—informally of course. A very intelligent little boy, as was clearly proved by study and tests of his development up to the age of seven years, he was already definitely aware of difficulty in hearing when first seen. Very frequently he would say "pardon", showing that he had missed what was said and wanted to be able to follow it. No doubt this led to a speaker raising his or her voice, also Barry had begun spontaneously to lipread when given the opportunity. At this stage he relied very much on lipreading. Under guidance in the Clinic his mother learned to use a hearing and speech training aid with him at home and, when helped by it, he came to rely more on hearing and less on lipreading.

A key fact about Barry's audiogram is that, very soon after being introduced to use of the speech training aid, he always

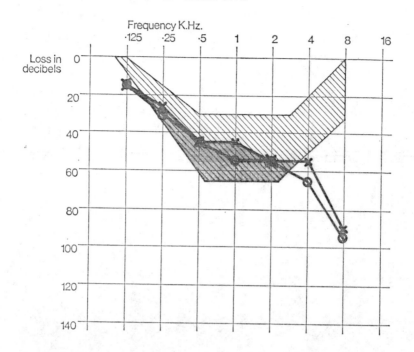

FIG. 3. Pure-tone audiogram of Barry without hearing aid

wanted its volume control set to give maximum output. When, on one occasion, his mother preferred to reduce the loudness level at which her speech reached Barry's ears (by about 10 decibels) he at once returned to his previous habit of saying "pardon" and ceased to do so when the loudness level was restored to maximum. The next diagram is intended to illustrate what must have been the reason. It is based on laboratory tests of the performance of auditory and speech training aids of high quality from which it is usual to find that they give good, high-fidelity amplification up to a frequency of about 5,000 cycles per second. The loudness level at which Barry's mother would usually speak into the microphone has been taken into account. It will be seen from the diagram

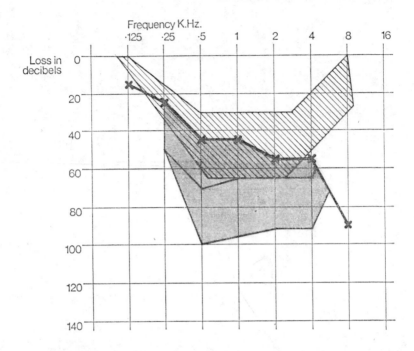

65 db speech

Speech area with broad-band speech trainer

FIG. 4. Pure-tone audiogram of Barry with speech training aid

that with the speech training aid almost the whole of the speech area could be made available to Barry.

The question now is "Could Barry be given facility to hear sound covering the whole or almost all of the speech area when using a body-worn hearing aid?" Certain problems at once present themselves. So far we have been evaluating what he could hear in quiet conditions in the clinic or home, with a portable, high fidelity hearing aid. But in ordinary life there are many conditions which are more difficult. First there is the amount of background noise present. Ordinary listeners to television and radio programmes are sometimes acutely aware of the difficulty that background noise can cause to hearing speech distinctly. This

111

is in spite of having unimpaired hearing. It can happen that the same kind and amount of noise may cause more difficulty in this respect when electronically transmitted and reproduced than it does when listening, on the spot, to the speech and the noise reaching our ears directly from their sources. Partly this is because, when present on the spot, we are using BINAURAL HEARING. This means that since particular sounds reach each of our ears separately as it were, at slightly different times and with slightly different loudness the wonderful mechanism of the brain is able to give us useful help in sorting out the speech from the noise.

Then there is the point that electronic amplification, even at its best, tends to distort sound. In many places ordinary school classrooms have been proved by acoustic experts to be a notable example. Reverberation is a sound distorting factor. The term ACOUSTIC IMPRINT has been coined to describe changes in sound patterns caused by noise and reverberation. That is why classrooms and sometimes other parts of school buildings especially designed for deaf and hard of hearing children, wearing hearing aids, are sound treated with acoustic tiles, etc.

Another point is that the comparatively low-pitched sound that constitutes a great deal of that found in ordinary noises tends very much to MASK crucial parts of the sound of speech. There is a physiological reason why loud background noise, even when not actually louder than the speech sounds, may impair the ability to hear them. There are very valuable tape recordings of speech, as reproduced by body-worn hearing aids, in typical background noise and typical amounts of reverberation, which we have found capable of demonstrating to audiences with unimpaired hearing the difficulty that hearing aid users are up against.

When considering the possibilities for a child of a body-worn, or for that matter an ear level hearing aid, to be used continuously all and every day by a young child, it is not enough to take account only of the sound of speech, as it reaches the microphone, in a very quiet room. In all other conditions the factors just discussed change and complicate, in varying degrees, the amplified sound available to the child. One technique for reducing the impact of noise and reverberation on the intelligibility of speech as heard through hearing aids has been to give greater amplification to the upper half of the speech range of frequencies than to the lower half. The influence in this direction,

in Great Britain, of post-war research under the auspices of the Medical Research Council and, in the U.S.A. of post-war research in the Psycho-Acoustic Laboratory at Harvard University, has been very considerable. There is a number of contemporary hearing aids, internationally available, that provide a similar type of amplification, by means of tone controls or specifically designed earphones or a combination of both.

It may be helpful to quote a few noise levels, typical of modern urban conditions, in relation to the DECIBEL SCALE of intensities used in audiograms. This scale has to cover, as well as degrees of hearing impairment, the enormous range of loudness of sound experienced in ordinary life. For this reason a sound twenty decibels greater in intensity than another is a hundred times greater, a difference of thirty decibels means a thousand times and sixty decibels a million times. Examples are: a quiet room in a private house noise level below 40 decibels: a busy restaurant, sound treated, 66–70 decibels: an electric vacuum sweeper at 6 feet 75 decibels: in a medium-sized car at 40 m.p.h. 82 decibels.

A critical point for hearing-aid users is the way in which speakers, quite unconsciously, adjust the loudness levels of their voices to be heard, by normal listeners, in relation to the amount and nature of the noise that is present. In a quiet room, for instance, with noise level below 40 decibels, we have found typical speech levels to be at 6 feet 52 decibels and at 20 feet 42 decibels. By contrast, in a busy restaurant, with noise level 66–70 decibels, the speech level at 3 feet was increased to 70–76 decibels. Variations in the loudness of speech reaching the microphones of hearing aids are known to affect their performance. To make available their maximum output a sound level of 70 decibels at the microphone is sometimes quoted. This level is somewhat greater than that recognised as typical of average conversational speech at 3 feet. It is relevant here to ask our readers to think about the loudness and quality of voice and speech used by professional newscasters. In the U.K., at any rate, news bulletins are normally read more loudly and with more careful articulation than is usual in casual conversation. This is in spite of the fact that the electronic equipment used in television and radio systems is definitely superior to that which can be included in body-worn hearing aids. The bulletins are being read within a short distance of the microphones and the studios are fully sound protected.

Finally, among problems that have to be faced in planning use of hearing aids for children under five there is the vital factor that affects all young children in their age range, those with normal hearing as well as the hearing impaired. Every child has to pass through a stage of learning to discriminate the sound patterns of the spoken language used by the people amongst whom he lives. For normal children, of course, the process of learning this skill is spread over the first five years of life and to some extent even beyond that. At the same time a child is learning the kinds of words, the kinds of phrases and sentences that belong to his native language.

All unhandicapped children, while first learning their native language, depend upon having much experience of hearing complete sound patterns of words and sentences. When considering provision of hearing aids for deaf children under five years this has to be taken into account, as well as the fact that, like their unhandicapped compères, they have to gather all the skill that they can in auditory discrimination through experience. A great contrast exists between their situation and that, say, of a deafened adult who needs a hearing aid. With all his past experience of language and accumulated auditory skill, he can usually fill in the gaps if he only partly hears a sentence. For instance, there are words and syllables in every sentence that are not given emphasis. They are spoken less loudly than those that are given it. A very simple example is the sentence "*I'm going to take the dog for a walk*". Normally, the syllables and words in italics would be given *stress* or emphasis and so be spoken more loudly, with longer duration than those unstressed. Young deaf children, aware only of the stressed syllables and words, have often been heard to speak sentences like this in the incomplete form "I go take dog walk." The mind of a deafened adult fills in gaps such as those. In conditions of part hearing, his mind can fall back on probabilities. This applies also to the ways in which particular vowels and consonants are fitted together to make words in a language, e.g. in English /h/ is spoken at the beginning and in the middle of words like *head* and *ahead* but in Arabic also at the end as in the name *Fatta'h*. There is an obvious contrast between the French and English languages in the use of the consonant, sometimes written as /zh/. In French this consonant is used at the beginning of words—je (I), jamais (never), jeune

(young). In English we do not meet this. The consonant /zh/ is used in middle positions in words—television, measure, seizure.

We give these few examples to illustrate the fact that every child, acquiring his native language, has to learn quite unconsciously the ways in which vowels and consonants are put together to make words and the ways in which words are put together to form phrases and sentences. Of course, children do not begin by listening to vowels and consonants as separate entities. It is to the meaning of words, usually in simple sentences, that their attention is primarily directed. Proof that their auditory discrimination of the sound patterns of words and sentences that they are learning to understand is often at first incomplete is given very clearly by some of the mispronunciations that all underfives at times utter. Mothers often say to us about their normally hearing children, when very young, "I understand him but other people don't". These are stages through which hearing-impaired children with greater or lesser potential capacity for auditory discrimination have to pass. As regards hearing aids our objective has always been to make opportunities for them to learn to hear as accurately as their handicap permits and, of course, in situations meaningful to them.

A body-worn aid, when duly prescribed in an audiology clinic, is the only means by which a child who needs amplification can have it made available to him at all times. For underfives, learning to talk at home and at school, acoustic conditions matter even more than for any other group of hearing aid users. They are of particular importance to a child who has to become accustomed, for the first time, to use an aid. We want sound patterns to reach him with the least possible amount of distortion, acoustic-imprint. Our method of introducing children under five to amplification, by using an auditory speech training aid, has been described earlier. With some children it has proved best to follow that method before beginning with a body-worn aid. In any case, it is highly advisable to ensure quiet conditions, whenever practicable, in the home, for some time after the child has started to wear an aid.

The proportion of the speech area, that is the extent to which the sound patterns of speech can be made available to children with body-worn aids, varies both in individual cases and with different hearing aids. For Barry, as the next diagram shows,

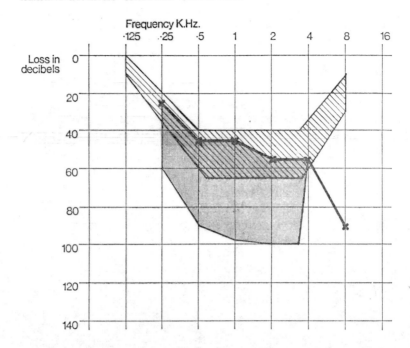

65 db speech

Speech area with body-worn aid

FIG. 5. Pure-tone audiogram of Barry with a body-worn aid

there are body-worn hearing aids which, in quiet conditions and with a clear speaker, would open up to him most of the speech area. To achieve this, good microphone techniques have to be used by a speaker and the volume control of the hearing aid adjusted to suit Barry.

Next, let us look at the audiograms of two of the more severely deaf children, under five years of age, whose histories have been given in full in Chapter One.

The audiogram of Sally, Fig. 6, makes clear the reason why, when first seen, she was neither vocalising nor responding to speech. Without amplification hardly any sound of typical conversational speech, even at only three feet, was audible to her,

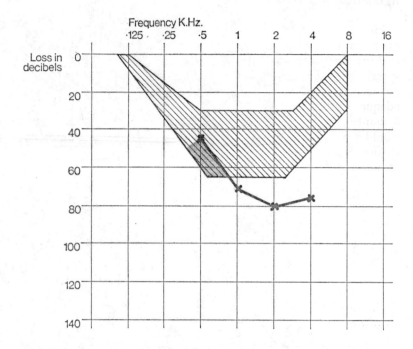

FIG. 6. Pure-tone audiogram of Sally without hearing aid

probably a little intermittent low-pitched sound of voice. It would seem so faint that it would be unlikely to be noticeable to her.

With a body-worn hearing aid of somewhat powerful type most of the speech area could be made available to her, as is shown in the next diagram, in ideal conditions. It was clear from laboratory tests that for the hearing aid to perform at its very best speech would have to reach the microphone of the aid at greater loudness than is typical of average conversation at three feet. Using a body-worn aid like this in a quiet room, at a distance of six feet from a speaker, Sally could hear very much less of the essential sound patterns unless the speaker raised his voice. With someone talking at the quiet conversational level of 50 decibels (see p. 113) even with this very good type of hearing aid she would be unable to hear little if any sound in the lower frequency half of the speech range. With a broadband speech trainer, which helped her so invaluably, we did not find it possible for Sally to hear an adequate sound pattern of the consonant /s/. By age 3 years 8 months, in words that had become very familiar to her, she would use it correctly. From others she would omit it altogether. Figures 7 and 8 show how most of the speech area could be made available to Sally with the body-worn hearing aid, in ideal conditions, but still more of it with the speech trainer offering all the advantages obtainable from speaking close to microphones.

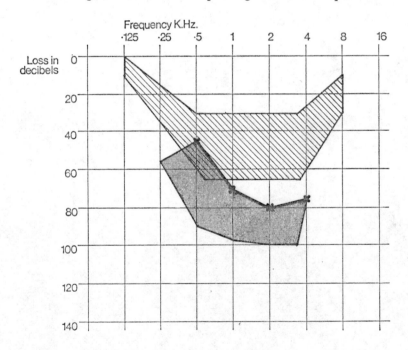

FIG. 7. Pure-tone audiogram of Sally with body-worn aid

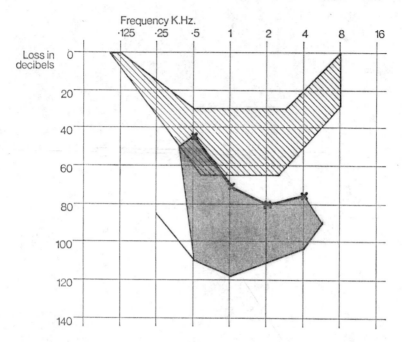

65 db speech

Speech area with broad-band speech trainer

FIG. 8. Pure-tone audiogram of Sally with speech training aid

Sheila, as we have already reported in Chapter One, was a child whose parents were able to give her very successful home training indeed, beginning at the age of fourteen months. She was profoundly deaf. This was established by a series of tests. The audiogram, Fig. 9, was taken at the age of 3 years 11 months. It indicated only too clearly that without amplification speech was inaudible to her in any ordinary real life situation.

A body-worn aid of the type that was adequate for Sally could not give Sheila enough help. Figure 10 illustrates the fact that with a special, different type of body-worn hearing aid, commercially available, much of the speech area could be amplified enough to be audible to Sheila. The diagram is related to a type

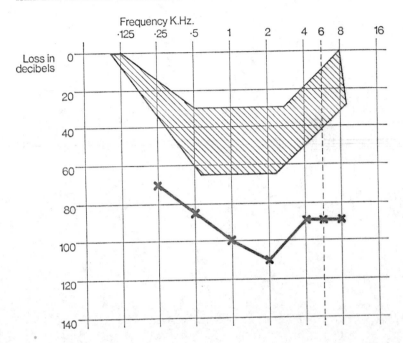

65 db speech

No speech area without aid

FIG. 9. Pure-tone audiogram of Sheila without aid

of hearing aid designed to meet the need of very severely deaf children. It is particularly suitable for those better able to hear sound in the lower than the higher frequencies.

The extent of the speech area available to Sheila with an auditory and speech training aid, significantly greater, is indicated in Fig. 11.

When a body-worn hearing aid is prescribed for their child parents are informed about EAR-MOULDS. They see that these are essential to the use of the hearing aid and have to be made for each child individually. It is usually advisable to have two ear-moulds, one for each ear. Three things are essential and parents need to be aware of them. First, they have to be shaped so that

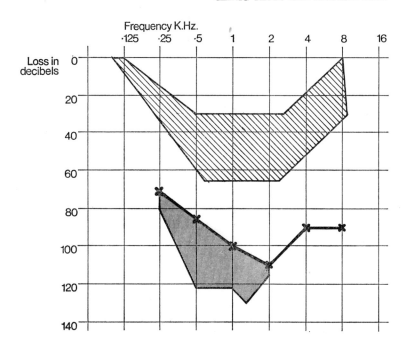

FIG. 10. Pure-tone audiogram of Sheila with special body-worn aid

they are kept in position whatever head movements the hearing-aid user makes. The part of the ear-mould that ensures this is sometimes described as the clip. Second, the whole pattern of the ear-mould, including the tube part that conveys the sound from the hearing-aid receiver into the ear canal, has to be very well fitting. Third, there is, of course, the importance of the ear-mould being comfortable to the wearer.

In fact the efficiency of a hearing aid depends very much indeed on the ear-mould. If it fails to fit exactly, sound leaks out through any gap left between it and the ear. The worst feature of this is when the leaked sound is picked up by the microphone of the hearing aid and, being amplified again, causes a whistling, squeal-

9

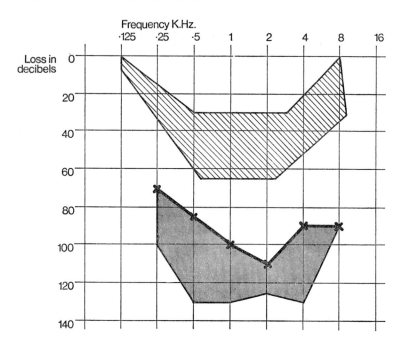

 65 db speech

Speech area: broad-band speech trainer

FIG. 11. Pure-tone audiogram of Sheila with speech training aid

ing noise. This is called an ACOUSTIC FEED-BACK. It can be reduced, sometimes stopped altogether, by turning down the volume control of the hearing aid. Particularly in cases of severe deafness the net result is only too often a lowering of the amplification below the level needed by the user.

To provide very young children, particularly babies, with exactly fitting ear-moulds requires much expertise. Sometimes a second impression or processing or both are necessary. Children's ears grow in size and for this reason ear-moulds have to be replaced at varying intervals of time.

From research on hearing-impaired children of school age it seems clear that for many of them there is a definite level of loudness at which they hear best. More than quite a moderate increase of sound intensity, as well as a reduction of it, prevents these children from hearing equally well. In Chapter Four we have described our method of trying to find a very young child's BEST HEARING LEVEL. Designers of auditory and speech training aids usually facilitate this by providing numbered intervals on the volume control for each ear. With some makes of body-worn hearing aids, including the British National Health Service Medresco aid, this help is also available. In such cases the volume setting of a body-worn aid, under expert guidance, can be adjusted with a considerable degree of precision in relation to a child's pure-tone audiogram.

In this connection a mention should be made of the fairly recently developed apparatus called the FREE-FIELD AUDIOMETER. Specially designed for hearing tests of very young children, this is held at a prescribed distance from each ear in turn, on a level with it. Our own method of using a free-field audiometer in a clinical test of infants is identical with that which we have described in Chapter Two, for making screening tests of children in the seven to nineteen months age-group. The child is alerted and brought to a noticing state of attention by the "occupier", who collaborates closely with the tester. This technique obtains responses to sound by young children at significantly lower intensities than those needed to evoke a startle response.

The positioning of a body-worn hearing aid can affect considerably the amount of help that it gives. For children, it has long been usual to provide HEARING AID HARNESSES. Made with various materials, these are designed to keep a hearing aid fixed in a suitable position on a child's body. Almost always that position is high up on the chest with the microphone itself uncovered. A majority of underfives, for whom hearing aids are prescribed, have an urgent need to hear their own voices amplified, i.e. through their hearing aids. It is just as essential for them to hear their own voices through their body-worn aids as it is for them to hear themselves vocalise and talk through an auditory and speech training aid. One has to remember that children's voices are not always very strong. Even with the microphone high up on his chest there is likely to be a falling off in the intensity of his voice of 20–25 decibels, before it reaches it, as contrasted with the loudness of his voice when leaving his lips.

It is very advisable for parents and teachers to have information as to what a child can hear with a particular body-worn aid at real life distances. In the February, 1968, number of the *Volta Review*, Dr. Daniel Ling of McGill University and Mrs. Doris Leckie of the Montreal Oral School for the Deaf reported that they had tackled this problem with twelve children who had residual hearing mainly restricted to low frequencies. With a standard model hearing aid (amplifying from 250 to 3,000 cycles per second), the vowel /ee/ was only audible up to about three feet although they could hear the vowel /ah/ at thirty feet. With one of the more recently developed type of body-worn aids (amplifying from 100 to 3,000 cycles per second) all vowels and voiced consonants were audible to all the twelve children at 35–40 feet. This is the kind of hearing aid, whose capacity to benefit children like Sheila we have illustrated in Fig. 10. In our experience, there are a good many children to whom this special type of body-worn hearing aid will give an almost continuous version of speech sound, whereas with the usual type only occasional patches of speech sound may be audible.

Tests made by ourselves, with a number of special school children using body-worn aids, showed that they could hear best a speaker who was in front of them. In the same conditions and at the same distance of nine feet but from either side speech was heard less well. Some findings by one of the world's greatest authorities on hearing, Professor Georg von Békésy of Harvard University, led us to make these tests. He reported that speech is best heard when uttered directly from in front of a listener and by someone turned to face him. Needless to say, speech from behind a hearing aid user is a cause of disadvantage.[1] The sound has to travel round his body which in itself absorbs a good deal of its energy before it reaches the microphone of his hearing aid.

Some readers may wonder why, so far, we have made no mention of EAR-LEVEL AIDS. Worn on the head, behind the ear, they pick up sound at the normal head position. Their size and weight are small. Unlike body-worn hearing aids they have no flexes or little cables, connecting the main unit with the receiver at the ear, which need to be arranged through or under outer clothing and up the neck. There is no possibility of CLOTHES RUB. This is

[1] This refers to body-worn aids.

noise caused by friction of clothing against the case of a body-worn aid as the user moves about and amplified by it.

Supply of ear-level hearing aids, to large numbers of hearing-impaired school children, was first reported from Denmark and in Britain from the Inner London Education Authority. For children under five years we believe that their use is impractical. They are too easily displaced and only too easily damaged. Because their volume controls have to be minute they are difficult for parents or teachers to adjust to any desired setting. They cannot be manipulated at all, while these hearing aids are in use, without bringing a hand close to a child's head, which involves drawing his attention to what, at first, may seem to him to be that strange thing on his ear. With other hearing aids, by the age of five years, it is not unusual for children themselves to learn to adjust volume controls. Such adjustments are necessary when a hearing aid user moves from quiet conditions to a noisy background or vice versa. Smallness of the controls of ear-level aids makes this difficult.

In their most vital years of learning to develop their hearing potential and learning to talk, it is of paramount importance for underfives to have as much experience as can possibly be contrived of using their hearing aids in really quiet conditions. But there are all the other times when noise of different kinds and different degrees of loudness is inevitably present. It can be a great help for a speaker to be much nearer to the microphone than the source of noise. This can be a way of contriving that speech is reproduced with greater intensity than background noise. The relationship between the two is technically described as the SIGNAL-NOISE RATIO. Readers will have seen outside broadcasters apply the technique. The setting of a volume control to match a child's best hearing level for speech can amplify background noise to a sound level that masks sound patterns that he needs to hear. For one thing, there is a limit to the level of intensity of sound that a hearing aid, particularly a body-worn aid or an ear-level aid, can reproduce without distortion. As we have already stated, an input sound level of 70 decibels is optimum for some aids.

More important still, human ears can be overloaded. In deafness due to certain causes this can have the result that the mechanism of hearing distorts sound patterns although they have reached the ear with good fidelity. It is very advisable for a parent, a teacher or anyone else responsible for underfive hearing aid users to discuss with an expert the varied acoustic conditions that the child meets in daily life with a view to adjusting the aid accordingly. Tone controls can be useful to some children. So also can be AUTOMATIC VOLUME CONTROL. In places like a very noisy city street, a fairground, a playground or even at times in a play-group, it may be best to switch off the aid altogether. Noise can damage hearing.

Perhaps it would be helpful to close this chapter with a summary of the microphone techniques that we recommend:

(1) Voice—Strength of voice to produce a hearing aid's best performance has to be greater than most people use in quiet, casual conversation. One good way of coming to appreciate this particular microphone technique is to listen discriminatingly to the best professional broadcasters. To drop one's voice, say at the end of a sentence, is something to avoid. It was shown long ago, by laboratory tests, that the resonant, more musical voices come across better. It is natural, of course, for voices to vary but with careful thought and attention many can be improved.

(2) Clear Speech—All hearing aid users are helped by being spoken to unhurriedly and with articulation that is distinct—without slurrings or omissions, particularly of consonants. Even with the youngest children sentences or phrases are always to be preferred to single words. To the hearing aid user, as well as the lipreader, they are pretty certain to offer more cues. It seems highly probable, also, that for young hearing-impaired children duration of an utterance matters. Naturally, length of sentence has to be adjusted to children's ages and state of development. This applies also to choice of vocabulary.

(3) Positioning—Whenever possible, be in front of the child so as to give the sound of one's speech a direct unimpeded pathway from the lips to the microphone. This facilitates what we have found always to be helpful—opportunity for a child to develop the special skill of combining such cues as he can possibly be given through electronic amplification with those cues that can be made visible to him as a lipreader. He needs

to be able to see all of a speaker's face, including the eyes. After all, changes in facial expression provide one set of cues. Both as a microphone technique and for lipreading one has to contrive, on every possible occasion, that one's face is on a level with a young child's.

(4) Ear to Voice Link—Continuous consideration and observation needs to be made as to whether a child is hearing his own voice and his own speech, when he has begun to talk. The microphone of his aid should *never* be more than nine inches from his lips.

7

Especially for parents

Having read the earlier chapters of this book you may feel that you have problems which have not yet been discussed. We hope that you are now convinced, if you were not already so beforehand, that you want to give your hearing-impaired child the best possible chances in life—most important of all that he should enter upon his rightful heritage of learning to talk. About this, to whatever nation you belong and wherever it is that you live, there can be no delay.

Once a hearing impairment in a child has been professionally confirmed what matters most is to get on with the job of finding out how he can best be helped. Of course, we have met parents who have spent much time and thought trying to trace out responsibility for a child's deafness. The best answer to this was given by a father who said to his wife "It doesn't matter who is responsible. It is our child. We're in this together and we must do our best for him." And that is just what they did. We all hope that advances in medical science will continue to prevent more and more of the handicaps that are found among young children. As yet there are still causes of hearing impairment that cannot be prevented and many of the world's children continue to be unexpectedly handicapped by some of them.

Sometimes, quite often indeed, it is parents who are the first people to suspect that their child is not hearing normally. None the less, to have their fears confirmed by medical diagnosis administers a shock that is very painful indeed. For those who never suspected deafness as a cause, say, of backwardness in learning to talk, or as a result of a child's illness, the shock can be even greater. The first thing is to make sure of using all available professional assistance and support. At the time of the consultation parents may be too mentally stunned to understand and realise the practical implications of the diagnosis. A later opportunity for parents to discuss the medical and audiological findings in a clinic or during a home visit should not be too long delayed. Delay in acceptance of a child's deafness simply means continued deprivation for him. It is he who has to live with it. Parents will always find, we believe, that personal and individual guidance about the home training of their children is the best thing. The medical consultant who has made the diagnosis will usually tell them where to get it. There are national and international centres from which help is always most gladly made available, such as the National Deaf Children's Society and the Royal National Institute for the Deaf in London, the Alexander Graham Bell Association for the Deaf, Washington D.C., and the Association Française des Communautés d'Enfants in Paris.[1]

There are three kinds of practical problem which are common to most parents who are seeking to give home training to their hearing-impaired children. They come under the three headings of time, space and relationships within the family.

First of all, time. There are the two kinds of training that need attention. It is so important to make use of daily routines to develop the child's capacity for communication and for co-operation in practical activities in relation to his stage of maturity. Our methods to achieve these objectives have been described in detail earlier in this book. Inevitably this means spending more time on routines like dressing and bathing and going to bed, getting ready to go out, meals, helping round the house when old enough and so on. It requires much patience and extra effort on the mother's part every now and then to interrupt what she is intent on doing and to concentrate her mind on effective communication with him, positioning herself so that he can best hear and see what she is saying. We know so well that to do this day after day is very demanding on a busy housewife. This may mean that for a few years she has to become less house-proud. Her husband and family need to be led to understand clearly the reasons for that. Time is required, also, for the special periods with special toys and special use of amplification, preferably with an auditory training unit, as described in Chapter Four. Accord-

[1] Addresses in full at the end of this Chapter.

10

ing to the age of the child they entail from ten minutes, several times a day with a baby, to twenty or thirty minutes, twice a day, for an older underfive.

When the hearing-impaired child has been the only child in the family it has not proved difficult to organise times for both aspects of home training. It is a very good thing, even essential, for father to take part in both, at weekends and during holiday periods. This is a key factor in building up a father–child relationship and inter-communication. It helps to prevent a very real risk of the hearing-impaired child's coming to depend too much on mother. By sharing responsibility father reduces the strain on mother as well as giving her effective moral support. Also it allows her more time for other matters.

Where there are other young children in the family, not yet at school, organisation of home training for the hearing-handicapped one becomes more difficult. For the special periods parents need to be free from interruptions. Where there is a younger baby the mother often finds it best to choose times when the baby is asleep in its cot or pram. A normally hearing toddler provides more problems. He may not be mature enough or willing to play alone quietly, outside the hearing-impaired child's field of vision. He will be curious about what is going on and will want himself to play with the toys. An older child can usually learn to understand why he needs to keep quiet without interfering but the toddler is unlikely to be ready for that. A neighbour may be able to let the toddler play with a child of her own for short periods. Where grandmothers or aunts live near enough they can be most helpful. One period a day may be taken by mother or father, when he is home from work. With practice and skill it is possible for a parent to bring the normally hearing toddler into the special training periods, learning to co-operate and alternate in play with the special toys. He can be prompted as to what he is to say to his sibling, through the microphone. The two children can be asked to push and roll things towards each other. The toddler can learn to keep quiet while mother has her turn.

Whatever the ages of siblings not yet at school, to bring them into the business of home training is most valuable. It has been surprising to see how well many of them can learn to attract a deaf child's visual attention when they want to say something to him and how accustomed deaf children, in these circumstances, have become able to understand what brothers and sisters say to them.

As a special treat, while all the children concerned are very young, unhandicapped brothers and sisters should be given occasional opportunities of playing with deaf children's special toys. This helps to avoid the risk of turning them into problem cases and of stirring up in them feelings of jealousy. If parents join in play with these toys it can help to dispel any impression that they are not as important or loved as much as the deaf sibling. It is equally good for the deaf child, in the family situation, to come to realise through actual experience that he has to share toys as well as his mother's attention. It will help all the children to become accustomed to give and take with each other.

There is no avoiding the fact that to give handicapped children home training demands an unusual amount of time and effort, both mentally and physically, from a mother. Fortunately, in most countries, this has only to be for a few years—until the children go to school, thus relieving the mother during many daytime hours. This fact of strain on mothers who give home training presents a cogent argument for provision of special schooling for hearing-impaired children who need it, in all countries, not later than at an age of three to four years.

At this point, perhaps, further emphasis should be given to the fact that in this book we are not urging acquisition of language just for its own sake. Very much more is at stake. Put quite simply, it is the whole emotional and social life of the child. When a deaf child and parents cannot talk to each other he is increasingly subject to feelings of frustration. Research has shown that for hearing-impaired children there is a greater risk of temper tantrums than for unhandicapped children. Conversely, there is evidence that deaf children have become less subject to temper tantrums as a result of a good early training that has given them spoken language with a wide vocabulary. They get past obtaining everything that they want by pointing to it and screaming if it is not given to them. Clearly they begin to develop a sense of security and confidence in their parents, as a result of having learnt to enjoy co-operative play with them and the give and take that is involved in the play-talk periods. Equally, parents achieve confidence and security in relationship with their children. The parents' initial fears, naturally common to many of them, of being unable to understand and manage their deaf children give place to satisfaction and a sense of achievement when the children make progress and successive difficulties are overcome.

From opportunities to follow up the subsequent careers of deaf children who were given good home training before the age of five years, we are convinced that the benefits to the growth of their minds and personalities stay with them through schooldays and on through adult life.

The value of regular, individual expert guidance to suit their particular conditions and needs, for all parents of hearing-impaired children, cannot possibly be overstressed. This is organised in different ways in various countries and in different districts. Where comprehensive provision is to be made as, for instance, is proposed in the United Kingdom by the Seebohm Report of 1969, it is inevitable that public authorities take financial responsibility.

Nowadays there is a problem for some mothers who feel that they have to earn money by going out to work. Put bluntly, the fact is that, if they can possibly afford to do so, they are very wise indeed to give up employment for the few years needed to undertake home training of a deaf child before he goes to school. In cases known to us in which this has been done rewards for both child and parents have been great and permanent.

Circumstances in which there is unavoidable necessity for a mother of a deaf child to have paid employment, for much of her time, are amongst those that, in Chapter Five, we have discussed as a reason for his going early to school. If efficient, regular training cannot be given at home a deaf child's need, by the time he has reached the age of two and a half years, is so urgent that there is no other alternative. When a mother has to go out to work she has to make some arrangement for the care of her child and special class or school is the best.

There are practical ways that have proved very helpful towards enabling little deaf children to settle down at school happily. For parents, also, they make it less difficult. The first step can be taken when the parent is initially faced with the possibility of a decision to accept a vacancy at school for her child—or a place on the waiting list. A visit to the school is arranged. By seeing for themselves how other children are happily occupied and by meeting the teachers, parents can realise how much the school has to offer. If it is a boarding school they can see the out-of-school accommodation with all the play facilities, and meet the matron. A very good thing is for them to take their child with them. Most schools, after a local authority has investigated a child's case and recommended his admission, desire to see him personally.

As regards preparation for going to school, non-home trained children are at a disadvantage. Absence or inadequacy of parent–child communication makes explanation impossible or very difficult. In such circumstances, it is particularly important for a mother, even though normally at work, to take her child to school for a day during the term previous to his admission. This applies, of course, to day schools or boarding schools when reasonably accessible. Most schools suggest and welcome this. If a mother is not staying all the time in the same room as her child she can leave, where he can see it, something of hers that he has come to associate with her. The child, if it seems desirable, can be shown where his mother is waiting. Many schools welcome and wish that such visits be made more than once. In this way a child becomes used to the teachers, other pupils and the building as well as to temporary separations from his mother and home.

At a child's first entry to a boarding school it is often the first night that is a difficulty. When the school authorities permit, it is advisable that his parents go to his bedroom with him, before they leave, unpack his night clothes and teddy bear or favourite toy, leaving them on the bed in which he is to sleep with the suitcase beside it. When bedtime comes there is an awareness in the child's mind that his mother knows where he is. In the practical experience of one of us, over many years, this plan has conduced greatly to children's sense of security.

Parents of weekly boarders need to school themselves to the possibility that their children may show signs of distress at being again parted from them after the first few weekends at home. Such upsets are often very short-lived. One means by which parents can be assured of this is by being permitted to wait somewhere or return a little while after leaving their child and see for themselves, perhaps through a window, without his being aware of their presence, that he has already settled down. Partings should not be prolonged. It is best to say goodbye quickly but not to disappear without the child knowing. Children should never be allowed to see or sense that their parents are feeling distressed. In the school of which one of us had charge, in cases where little children returned too late for play with other children before bedtime and evidenced exceptional emotional upsets at being separated from their parents, they settled down happily if their mothers or fathers were encouraged to put them to bed. Obviously, this could not be general practice for parents.

One of the risks for parents and others in bringing up deaf children is that of underestimating their potentialities in practical day-to-day matters. There has always been a tendency, partly perhaps due to difficulties in communication, to assume that the handicap of deafness causes backwardness in capacity for self-help, especially among underfives. There is a danger of trying to compensate for the children's deafness by doing for them things that they can readily learn to do for themselves. It may be helpful to refer, at this point, to composite tables which show the stages in progress of learning to feed and dress themselves found by eminent psychologists to be average for normal unhandicapped children:

Dressing

1 year	Holds out arm for sleeve or foot for shoe.
15 months	Likes to take off shoes.
18 months	Takes off gloves, socks, unzips.
	Tries to put on shoes.
2 years	Helps in dressing—finds large armholes and thrusts his arms into them.
	Helps to pull up or push down panties.
	Washes hands and dries them but does neither very well.
3 years	Greater help. Is able to unbutton front and side buttons. Apt to put pants on backwards, has difficulty in turning socks to get heels on. May put shoes on wrong feet. May need help with shirts and jerseys. Washes and dries hands. Brushes teeth with supervision.
4 years	Able to dress and undress with little assistance.
	Distinguishes back from front and puts clothes on correctly.
	Washes and dries hands and face. Brushes teeth.
5 years	Undresses and dresses with care.

Feeding

15 months Holds cup. Apt to tip it and spill. Needs close super-vision. Grasps spoon and inserts it into dish. Poor fill-ing of spoon. If brought to mouth is apt to turn upside down before entering mouth.

18 months Lifts cup to mouth and drinks well. Fills spoon, diffi-culty in inserting in mouth, apt to turn it in mouth. Considerable spilling.

21 months Handles cup well: lifting, drinking, replacing.

2 years Holds small glass in one hand as drinks. Inserts spoon in mouth without turning. Moderate spilling.

3 years Little spilling. Rarely needs assistance to complete a meal.

Besides the practical and social aspects of self-help for a young child there is the natural and valuable stimulation that such activities give to mental life as a whole. Intellectually a child is more active and less passive. He is relating himself and being more responsive to the world about him. For a deaf underfive who may have to go to boarding school ability to do things for himself adds to his sense of security on admission. Every step in this direction eases his parting from his parents.

Some parents whom we have known have worried greatly about helping their children to become socially adequate. For hearing-impaired as well as for other children the foundations for this are laid in the early years. Two main facts are involved. Like all children, those who are hearing-impaired can only become well-adjusted socially through experience of actual contacts with people, first in the home then, bit by bit, with others outside. The risk of social isolation through deafness has to be overcome and the earlier that a start is made about this the better. A second main fact is that a very spoilt child, accustomed from the be-ginning to get his own way if he only makes enough fuss, is not socially attractive and this point applies to relationships with other children and being accepted by them as a playmate on equal terms.

As soon as parents, under guidance, feel confident that they have begun to develop their hearing-impaired child's interest in play with them it is good to bring in other adults and teenagers. Simple explanations can be given and they can be shown how to

135

obtain responses in spite of the hearing handicap. It is always much better for relations and friends to be informed of a child's deafness but also, at the same time, for them to realise in practical ways that he has potentialities. This policy saves the child from being misjudged if his behaviour is unusual just because he does not understand some situations. It is our experience that people are generally very sympathetic about handicaps, particularly among little children. Deafness being invisible, they need to be informed about it.

How young children learn to play with one another is a subject that has been much studied by psychologists. A two-year-old usually likes to play by himself although he may be pleased to have other children around. At this age snatching and grabbing toys from the others is a perfectly normal characteristic. It is by the age of three years that he is spontaneously attracted to join up with a few others. In ordinary circumstances and on his own initiative the duration of a child's joint play with others may be short.

All this has practical implications for parents of a hearing-impaired child. If he is the only child, or the only one to be at home during the greater part of each day, co-operation of nearby relations and friends who have children of about the same age may be sought. Any group of underfives are helped to enjoy joint play much better by having an understanding adult at hand. When a deaf or hard of hearing child is one of the group such adult help can make all the difference. What has been written in this paragraph applies to methods of enabling hearing-impaired children to get the most possible benefit from being members of play groups.

There are some circumstances in which hearing impairment, because it is associated with some other form of severe handicap, makes special provision urgent and necessary. For a parent to be wholly responsible, all day and every day, for the care and training of a child like this imposes excessive and sometimes an impossible amount of strain. This is particularly true of children who are abnormally late in learning to walk and to feed themselves. Among histories of such children we have found medical diagnoses of severe cerebral palsy, mongolism with blindness, gargoylism and severe mental backwardness. Parents of children like these need urgently to be able to hand over responsibility for their children to trained workers for part of each day. Medical advice is essential as to how this can be arranged. The Rodney House clinic, quoted in Chapter Three of this book, is an example of what is required. Much greater provision of facilities of this kind is imperative. It could take the form of local centres. Parents need to press for their establishment.

Group meetings for parents can play a very important part. As occasions for sharing problems they have considerable therapeutic value. It is not until they attend a group meeting that some parents realise that they are not alone in having a deaf child. Free discussion among groups of parents, including informal questioning of clinic staff who are present, has proved a helpful way of relieving parents' anxieties and of spreading information in a relaxed atmosphere. Demonstrations with their own children, when they can be arranged, by parents who have already gained experience and skill in home training, give encouragement and hope to parents newly faced with the problem and those who are coming up against initial difficulties.

Parents themselves through their own associations have contributed greatly, and in our personal experience most generously, towards progress in work for hearing-impaired underfives.

National and international centres

Association Nationale des Communautés d'Enfants,
145 boulevard Magenta,
Paris—10.

International Parents' Organisation,
Alexander Graham Bell Association for the Deaf Inc.,
1537, 35th Street N.W.,
Washington D.C. 20007.

National Deaf Children's Society,
31 Gloucester Place,
London, W1H 4EA.

Royal National Institute for the Deaf,
105 Gower Street.
London, W.C.1.

The John Tracy Clinic.
806 West Adams Boulevard,
Los Angeles,
California 90007.

Bibliography

Anderson, U. M. (1967) "The Incidence and Significance of High-Frequency Deafness in Children". *American Journal of Diseases of Children* 113, 560–565.

Beck, J. (1967) *How to Raise a Brighter Child.* Fontana/Collins, London.

Békésy, G. von (1960) *Experiments in Hearing.* McGraw-Hill, London, Toronto, New York.

Boothroyd, A. M. (1967) "The Discrimination by Partially-Hearing Children of Frequency Distorted Speech". *International Audiology* 6, 2, 136.

Dale, D. M. C. (1967) *Deaf Children at Home and at School.* University of London Press.

Davis, H. and Silverman, S. R. (1960) *Hearing and Deafness.* 2nd edition. Holt, Rinehart & Winston Inc., New York.

Ewing, A. W. G. (1967 facsimile of 1930 ed.) *Aphasia in Children.* Haffner Publishing Co., New York.

Ewing, A. W. G. and Ewing, E. C. (1964) *Teaching Deaf Children to Talk.* Manchester University Press and Volta Bureau, Washington 7, D.C.

Ewing, A. W. G. and Ewing, I. R. (2nd edition, 1961) *New Opportunities for Deaf Children.* University of London Press.

Fletcher, H. (1953) *Speech and Hearing in Communication.* Van Nostrand, New York.

Fellendorf, G. W. and Harrow, H. (1970) "Parent Counselling 1961–1968". *Volta Review,* 72, 1, 51–57.

Gesell, A. (1940) *The First Five Years of Life.* Methuen, London.

Gilmore, M. E. (1970) "Speechreading in Kindergarten". *Special Education in Canada* 44, 2, 23–25.

Griffiths, R. (1954) *Abilities of Babies.* University of London Press.

Hardy, J. (1965) "The Etiology of Neonatal Deafness and the High-Risk Register", in *The Young Deaf Child: Identification and Management. Acta Oto-Laryngologica, Supplementum* 206, 66–69.

Hardy, W. G. (1965) "Evaluation of Hearing in Infants and Young Children", in Glorig, A. *Audiometry: Principles and Practice.* Williams & Wilkins, Baltimore.

Harold, B. B. (1957) "The Effects of Variations in Intensity on the Capacity of Deaf Children and Adults to Hear Speech with Hearing Aids". Unpublished Ph.D. thesis. Manchester University Library.

Harris, G. M. (1963) *Language for the Pre-School Deaf Child.* 2nd edition. Greene & Stratton Inc., New York.

Harris, G. M. (1964) "For Parents of Very Young Deaf Children". *Volta Review*, 66, 1, 19–26.

Huizing, H. C. (1960) "Potential Hearing in Deaf Children, its Early Development and Use for Auditory Communication". *The Modern Educational Treatment of Deafness* (ed. Ewing). Manchester University Press.

Illingworth, R. S. (1960) *The Development of the Infant and Young Child.* Livingstone, Edinburgh and London.

Leckie, D. and Ling, D. (1968) *Audibility with Hearing Aids having Low Frequency Characteristics. Volta Review* 70, 2, 83–86.

Markides, A. (1970) "Symptoms of Recruitment Shown by Pre-School Hearing-Handicapped Children". *Sound* 4, 2, 50–52.

Masland, R. L. (1968) "Rubella Can Rob Children of their Hearing". *Volta Review*, 70, 5, 304–307.

McCarthy, D. (1954) "Language Development in Children", in Carmichael L., *Manual of Child Psychology.* John Wiley & Sons Inc., New York. Chapman & Hall, London.

Oppé, T. E. (1967) "Risk Registers for Babies" *Developmental Medicine and Child Neurology*, 9, No. 1.

Overgaard, J. (1968) "Identification of the Young Deaf Child, Types of Tests Used at Danish Hearing Centres". *Féderation international des Communautés d'Enfants, Document* 13, 135–145.

Robson, J. (1970) "Screening Techniques in Babies". *Sound*, 4, 4, 91–94. Royal National Institute for the Deaf, London.

Sanders, D. A. (1971) *Aural Rehabilitation.* Prentice-Hall Inc., New Jersey and Prentice-Hall International Inc., London.

Sheridan, M. D. (1960) *The Development Progress of Infants and Young Children.* H.M. Stationery Office, London.

Simmons, A. A. (1966) "Language Growth for the Pre-Nursery Deaf Child". *Volta Review*, 68, 3, 201–205.

Taylor, I. G. (1964) *The Neurological Mechanisms of Hearing and Speech in Children.* Manchester University Press and Volta Bureau, Washington 7, D.C.

Taylor, I. G. (1970) "Diagnosis of Conductive and Perceptive Deafness in the Pre-School Child". *International Audiology*, 9, 1, 140–141.

Uden, A. M. J. van (1968) *A Maternal Reflective Method.* Institute for the Deaf, St. Michielsgestel, Holland.

Veit, P. (1968) "Appareilage Précoce et Pré-Scholaire: Selection et Adaptation de la Prothése Auditive Individuelle." *Federation international des Communautés d'Enfants, Document* 13, 183–194.

Watson, T. J. (1967) *The Education of Hearing-Handicapped Children.* University of London Press.

Wedenberg, E. (1965) "Parental Skills and Attitudes, including Home Training", in *The Young Deaf Child: Identification and Management. Acta Oto-Laryngologica, Supplementum* 206, 203–206.

Wepman, J. M. (1960) "Outline of Auditory Discrimination Theory". *Elementary Schools' Journal,* 60, 325–333.

Whetnall, E. and Fry, D. B. (1964) *The Deaf Child.* Heinemann, London.

Index